ADVANCE PRAISE FOR

Never
Letting
GO

This is a book that should be read not only by
beginning and advanced students of life, but
by anyone who needs an uplifting message of
love, hope, and renewal. This deep, emotionally
touching book may well be destined to become
a metaphysical classic.

—Joyce Keller,
author of *Seven Steps to Heaven*
and *Calling All Angels*

Mark Anthony takes us on an enlightening
journey through coping with grief and
discovering spiritual renewal. I highly
recommend this book!

—Jeffrey A. Wands,
author of *Another Door Opens*

Mark Anthony has that rare ability to convey
inspirational information of hope along with the
determination of a seeker of truth. Mark's quest
to find answers has led him to revelations that can
help so many. Fascinating and enlightening.

—Robert Brown,
author of *We Are Eternal*

Never
Letting
Go

*M*ark Anthony has practiced law for over twenty years and has been a regular guest legal commentator on the Fox News Network. As a medium who studied at the prestigious Arthur Findlay College for the Advancement of Psychic Science in England, he has combined his intuitive gifts and his legal expertise to share insight and guidance with people coping with the aftermath of a life-threatening, life-changing, or life-ending trauma.

A member of the Florida Bar, US Supreme Court Bar, Washington DC Bar, and the Eleventh Judicial Circuit Bar, Mark graduated from Mercer University Law School with honors and studied law at Oxford University in England. Through his numerous lectures and call-in media interviews, he has helped thousands of people better understand the afterlife. He lives in Florida. For more information about Mark Anthony, visit his website at www.healgriefwithbelief.com.

NEVER LETTING GO

Heal Grief with Help from the Other Side

MARK ANTHONY

Llewellyn Publications
WOODBURY, MINNESOTA

First Edition
Eighth Printing, 2019

Book design by Rebecca Zins
Cover image © 2011 iStockphoto.com/Hougaard Malan
Cover design by Ellen Lawson

Llewellyn is a registered trademark
of Llewellyn Worldwide Ltd.

Library of Congress Cataloging-in-Publication Data
Anthony, Mark, 1960–
   Never letting go: heal grief with help from the other side / Mark
Anthony.—1st ed.
      p. cm.
   ISBN 978-0-7387-2721-9
1. Spiritualism. 2. Grief. 3. Bereavement. I. Title.
BF1272.A58 2011
   133.9'1—dc23

                                                        2011023512

Llewellyn Publications
A Division of Llewellyn Worldwide Ltd.
2143 Wooddale Drive
Woodbury, MN 55125-2989
www.llewellyn.com

Printed in the United States of America

This book is dedicated to my beloved mother, Jeannie,
a woman who made a positive difference in so many lives
when she was here in the material world and who
continues to do so from the Other Side.

Thanks, Mom, for teaching me that love
really does transcend physical death.

Contents

Contents

The Prayer of Saint Francis

Lord, make me an instrument of your peace,
Where there is hatred, let me sow love;
Where there is injury, pardon;
Where there is doubt, faith;
Where there is despair, hope;
Where there is darkness, light;
Where there is sadness, joy;

O Divine Master, grant that I may not so much
  seek to be consoled as to console;
To be understood as to understand;
To be loved as to love.

For it is in giving that we receive;
It is in pardoning that we are pardoned;
And it is in dying that we are born to eternal life.

Grief is the price of love. You grieve as deeply as you loved ... Love is the great experience of life itself.

—Father Sonny

To Heal Grief,
Start with Belief

*W*hen you die, you really don't. The body may cease to function, but the soul is an immortal living spirit that continues to exist beyond physical life. Even with this understanding, coping with the death of a loved one is extremely painful. Spirits are aware of this and know bereaved loved ones here in the material world are suffering. That is why spirits will come to our emotional rescue by communicating with us.

Contact with a spirit can be an incredibly healing experience because it teaches us to let go of the sorrow caused by the death but hold on to the love for the person who died. Spirit contact also helps us understand that God exists, the Other Side exists, the soul is immortal, and we will be reunited with our loved ones when it is our time to leave this material world.

I'm often asked how I can be so sure of this. I certainly don't have all the answers—no one does—but I do have some insight. I am a psychic medium who was born with the ability to communicate with spirits.

I'm also a criminal defense and personal injury trial lawyer. I've represented thousands of people, many whose lives have been shattered by the deaths of loved ones. As a lawyer, I advise people that you can't change the fact someone you loved has died. What you can do is change your perspective on death. And with the help of spirits, that is what I do as a medium.

Many people seek my services as a medium to establish communication with the spirit of a loved one. Those who do have progressed to the point in their journey through grief where they believe it will be healing to communicate with the Other Side. In several instances, though, it is the spirits who choose the time and place of the contact. Sometimes, this occurs when you least expect it, as I discovered one day in my capacity as a lawyer during a jury trial.

I was representing a client who was accused of assault and battery. Jury selection is the beginning phase of the trial, which occurs before evidence is presented. The objective is to question a panel of prospective jurors to determine if they have any bias so both parties can obtain a fair and impartial jury. As I stood at the podium before the panel of jurors, I had an uneasy feeling about one of them. Prospective juror number nine was a nervous, middle-aged woman with a beautiful olive complexion, whom I'll refer to as "Juror Nine." My intuition about Juror Nine was confirmed when I became aware of a female spirit's presence near her. While it isn't unusual for me to perceive spirits, this wasn't the ideal time and place for a connection with the Other Side. I tried to ignore the spirit and continued on with my questioning of the jurors.

Since it was my obligation to seek out potential bias against my client, I asked Juror Nine, "Have you, or has anyone in your family, ever been the victim of a crime?"

She took a deep breath and then started to tremble. "Yes… about a year ago."

This information was important to the client I was representing since I had to ensure he would have an impartial jury. Apparently, this was also important to the spirit who wanted to communicate with Juror Nine, because my link with the spirit intensified. I felt a tightening around my throat, which indicated to me that the spirit had a problem breathing prior to her physical death. I continued, "What type of crime was that, if I may ask?"

"My sister was in a foreign country when an escaped mental patient strangled her. Then he dismembered her body and threw it in a dumpster—like she was garbage!" Juror Nine burst into tears as she covered her face with her hands.

I was aghast. The courtroom became extremely still. A few people gasped. One of the other jurors looked like he might become ill. Even the normally vociferous prosecuting attorney was temporarily speechless.

All eyes were upon me. Stunned and at a loss for words, I knew everyone expected me to do something. My professors in law school certainly hadn't taught me how to deal with this situation.

"I—I'm so sorry. I can't even imagine what you and your family have been through," came stumbling out of my mouth. "I wish I had the right words to console you."

"What could a lawyer possibly say to make me feel better?" Juror Nine replied bitterly.

"Please forgive me for bringing up such a painful memory," I responded.

"Painful? You have no idea what *painful* is," she said, struggling to regain her composure.

I wanted to move on, but Juror Nine was in agony, and her sister's spirit had come to her rescue. It was a huge risk personally and professionally, but I had to try. "Perhaps, if she were here, your younger sister would want you to know that her immortal soul lives on."

"They tell me that in grief counseling at my church. I'm sorry for being angry with you; it's not your fault. Please forgive me," Juror Nine said softly. "Maybe it's foolish, but I pray every day just to hear from my sister. Just to know she's okay."

A message from her sister's spirit resonated through me. I had to deliver it.

"Maybe when it comes to hearing from Heaven, sometimes *no news is good news.*" I relayed the message.

"No news is good news!" Juror Nine repeated excitedly as she sat up straight. "That's something we always said to each other! It was our secret inside joke. How in the world do you know that? Or that she was my little sister?"

"Objection!" boomed the prosecuting attorney.

"Sustained!" the judge ruled. "Mr. Anthony, I don't know what purpose this discourse is supposed to accomplish. Please move on to another juror."

Wiping the tears from her eyes with a tissue, Juror Nine looked at me and smiled gently. "Thank you; that made my day."

I AM OFTEN asked how I can be both an attorney and a medium at the same time. Having a foot in both worlds *is* challenging at times, yet I've never seen them as conflicting. Being both a medium and an attorney has proven beneficial to my clients over the years. I've also seen striking similarities between my dual professions.

Both of these careers are about helping people—to solve their legal problems or to ease their grief. In my legal and spiritual work, I've also seen how choosing the wrong means of dealing with death can devastate someone and the lives of those around that person. Finding the right path through grief is extremely important.

My dual professions are also evidentially based. As an attorney, I've been trained in critical thinking. I'm naturally skeptical and insist upon having verifiable evidence before accepting something as a fact. I apply the same type of critical thinking in my approach to mediumship. I require proof that the information I receive from spirits is accurate and real.

As a medium, I practice what is known as evidential mediumship. It is my job to present information and messages conveyed by a spirit. These details are the pieces of evidence conveyed from the Other Side to verify the validity of the contact for the recipient. In a way, it is like what I do in court. I present the evidence, and it is up to the jury to decide what to do.

In a mediumistic reading, I facilitate communication between a spirit and a person in the material world. It is the recipient of the message who is both the judge and the jury—and who decides what to do with the evidence presented by a spirit through me. Unfortunately, in both law and mediumship, sometimes the recipient doesn't listen to the message and is looking for what he or she wants to hear instead of what is communicated, but that is an individual's choice. My responsibility as a medium is to present the evidence and the information, not to dictate what a person does with it.

THE ABILITY TO communicate with spirits runs in my family. For at least a century, there have been psychics and mediums in both my mother's and my father's families. My mother, Jeannie Anthony, was particularly gifted, and I grew up in an environment where it was just as normal for my mother to see spirits as it was to see neighbors. She always seemed to know things other people didn't. She was an amazing and colorful woman who was something like a metaphysical combination of Shirley MacLaine, Lucille Ball, Ginger Rogers, and Elizabeth Taylor. My father once joked, "Add to that mix a touch of Muhammad Ali."

Throughout life, my mother always told me I was psychic. Of course, every mom tells her children they are talented and unique in some way. But if anyone could have known I was psychic, it would have been her.

FROM AN EARLY age, I would have dreams that later came to pass. Before I was five years of age, I had invisible friends who conversed with me. One afternoon, my sister, Roxanne, who was also my babysitter, asked, "Mark, who are you talking to?"

"The people," I said.

"What people? There's no one there."

"All those people." I pointed to where I sensed the presence of several spirits. "They're my friends." I was perplexed that she didn't see them.

My mother didn't have a problem with my invisible friends, but my father, Earl, did. When I was five years old, he told me, "Mark, don't talk to people who aren't there."

"Daddy, they *are* there," I insisted.

"They are not!" he said, turning up the volume of his voice.

My mother interjected, "Earl, leave him alone. He's not doing anything wrong."

"Jeannie, I don't want people thinking he's nuts!" he said, nervously pacing the room.

"Earl," my mother said softly, "maybe he's like us. You know what I mean."

My father came to a stop and faced her. "It's for his own good, Jeannie. I'm just trying to protect him."

When my father saw I was afraid, he spoke more calmly. "Mark, you scare people when you say things like that. People will think you're weird."

"I'm sorry, Daddy," I apologized.

My father explained, "Try to understand—people will make fun of you, and when you grow up, they'll say you're crazy. Weird adults who see things that aren't there get taken away. Please don't say you have invisible friends."

At the time, I couldn't understand why my father felt that way. Later, I learned that he too could perceive spirits, as could his sister, Margery. Sadly, in the early 1950s, Margery was subjected to public ridicule and enduring pain because she was open to the Other Side. She was forcefully taken away in a straightjacket to a mental institution and then subjected to electroshock therapy until she stopped using this gift. Understandably, this caused my father to fear and suppress his own innate spiritual connections.

SHORTLY BEFORE MY sixth birthday, I was enrolled in Catholic school, and my invisible friends seemed to appear less frequently. Perhaps I was taking Dad's advice. Maybe I was more preoccupied with school and the inevitable hours of homework that went with the rigors of Catholic schooling.

My psychic proclivity, though, did not diminish. I was always able to "read" people, and I remained sensitive to the presence of spirits, even though I didn't actively seek to communicate with them. My mother continued to openly discuss her psychic abilities, which I always found fascinating. She and I had a remarkable relationship; perhaps because I was her youngest, she felt especially close to me. From my earliest days, I always felt that our connection went beyond mother and son. We connected on a nonverbal level. She knew each time something went wrong in my life. Whenever I was having a difficult time, feeling frustrated and tempted to give up, she was there, or the phone would ring and there was Mom's voice, filled with concern and inspiring advice. She said when things were going badly for her, I always seemed to innately understand—I would just *know*, and there I was to comfort her. Despite this, I never fully embraced my abilities nor utilized them to their fullest extent until later in life.

THEN, ONE BREEZY and sunny Florida day, that changed. It was October 5, just after 9 AM. I was working as an attorney at the county courthouse. As I was about to leave the courtroom, the judge's secretary motioned to me.

"Attorney Anthony," she said quietly, "there's an urgent call from your secretary."

When I saw the look in her eyes, I knew it was going to be bad.

She led me to the judge's chambers. I stared down at the red light blinking ominously on the telephone, indicating a call holding for me. Slowly, I reached down and picked up the receiver.

"This is Mark Anthony."

"Mr. Anthony, your dad called ... he said your mom died."

Nothing had ever prepared me for the torrent of emotions that came next. The pressure in my head became unbearable. My skull felt as if it were exploding with every pulsing of my heart.

Mom can't be dead! She made me lunch yesterday! We had fun! She was fine!

Disbelief was quickly followed by a sick feeling that my stomach and chest were caving in. I put the phone down and heard myself say, "My mother died...you'll have to excuse me."

As I hurried out, I could hear the judge's assistant say, "I'm so sorry."

Attorneys must control their emotions. Despite years of discipline, the flood of feelings overwhelmed me. I fought to maintain composure while tears welled up in my eyes.

I had to get to my car. Adrenaline pumping, I flew down three flights of stairs in the courthouse. I rushed past people—some I recognized, others I didn't—their faces just a blur.

Next, full-blown <u>shock</u> set in. I felt detached from my body, and it seemed as if I were watching myself from the outside. My mind raced in different directions, hoping this wasn't real and that another call would come to tell me it wasn't true. Logic told me that call would never come.

When I arrived at my parents' house, it took all the fortitude I could command to walk through the front doorway. On the couch in the living room, covered by a blanket, lay my mother's lifeless body.

My brother, Earl Joseph, stood next to me. He is a rugged outdoorsman, always in control of his emotions. However, that day, even his iron discipline was buckling under the strain. With sorrow in his eyes, he explained, "The paramedics said she died peacefully in her sleep…I guess that's supposed to make us feel better."

That beautiful October day became the saddest period of my life.

Yet in loss there is gain, as in gain there is loss. On some level, though, I knew that this body wasn't really who she was. The mother I knew was somewhere else. But where?

A resolve arose within me. Someone I loved had disappeared, and I was determined to find her. I didn't care what I had to do or where I had to look, be it searching the earth or reaching out to Heaven. With God's help, I was going to do it.

Almost immediately, it became clear to me that to cope with my grief, I had to find a more positive understanding of death. During these dark days, the part of my brain which enables me to perceive psychic and mediumistic information, my so-called "third eye," opened. I now fully embraced my inherited abilities and found myself in the midst of amazing spiritual experiences. This awareness helped me to understand that to heal from grief, I had to have belief in God and in the existence of the Other Side.

As I started again on my journey to connecting with the Other Side, my mom's spirit was there with me, reassuring me that physical death is merely a steppingstone to the next level of our existence as an immortal spirit. The true nature and scope of our journey is far beyond anything we can really grasp here in the material world.

WHEN SOMEONE YOU love dies, nothing can change what has happened. Isolating yourself to brood over what you might have done differently won't change things. Taking drugs or drinking alcohol to numb yourself into oblivion temporarily dulls the pain but is unhealthy and can lead to addiction or sometimes to criminal activity. Jumping into a new relationship after a death to convince yourself that you are "over it" might be self-destructive financially and emotionally. There is no quick fix or magic potion to cure pain. The reality is that grieving takes time. Grief is not something you get over; it is something you go through. This is what I learned when my mother died. As I progressed through my grief, I came to accept the reality of her death and eventually found inner peace with her passing.

If dealt with properly, grief can lead to a positive outcome. It can transform the bereaved into a more compassionate, deeper, and sensitive person. A successful journey through grief may bring the gift of wisdom and cause a more developed sense of spirituality and a closer connection with God. Without a doubt, the most important tool for healing grief is *faith*.

Faith is trust and belief in a higher power. It is a dedication to the realization that there is a power greater than us through which all living things are connected. Faith brings us comfort in the knowledge that life is eternal and that our time in the material world is only temporary. Faith teaches that beyond this life there is something wonderful on the Other Side. The material world has no sorrow Heaven cannot heal.

I don't presume to tell anyone *how* to believe in the higher power—I just maintain that, in your own way, you *must*. The debate over which religion is the "correct" one has been going on since the dawn of time. Frustrated with unending quarrels between religions, Mahatma Gandhi once asked, "What religion is God?"

While visiting Japan, I was surprised to learn that it's typical for some people to be members of more than one religion. One can be a member of the Buddhist, Christian, and Shinto faiths all at the same time. Curious, I asked a Buddhist monk how this could be so. Serenely, he answered, "Who are we to put limitations upon the infinity that is God? There are as many paths to God as there are people in the world."

God exists in spite of religion, not because of it. Nonetheless, religion is still important. Religions teach that God exists and that the soul is immortal. Religious people who acknowledge that God is love and who do not use their faith as a moral pretext for hatred, anger, bigotry, or violence are truly on the path to enlightenment. God does not hate, but unfortunately people do. Hate is a negative emotion humans constantly seek to justify. God never justifies hate.

To free your heart and mind from hatred is to accept the love that is God. Hindus believe that when you look into the eyes of someone you love who loves you back, you are catching a glimpse of God. Christianity teaches us that one who does not love does not know God, for God is love.

Humanity has given God a host of names, such as Higher Power, Supreme Being, Yahweh, Christ, Brahman, Vishnu, Buddha, Jehovah, Allah, Great Spirit, Holy Spirit, the Source, and Infinite Light. Perhaps the spiritually oriented Beatle, George Harrison, had a point when he said, "All religions are branches of one big tree. It doesn't matter what you call God, just so long as you call."

MY GOOD FRIEND Father Sonny, a Catholic priest, once told me, "Grief is the price of love. You grieve as deeply as you loved." He continued, "Who would cast aside wonderful memories and love just to be spared the pain of grief? A life without love isn't much of a life at all. The fear of the pain of loss is no reason for one to be isolated from family, not to marry, not to have children, or not to extend one's heart to another. Love is the great experience of life itself."

The religions of the world teach us that when a person dies, the soul leaves the body to go to another realm. Reverend Val Williams of the Spiritualist National Union in the United Kingdom explains that people don't really die, "they simply move on to another dimension, divorced from all pain and all dissension." When a loved one dies, it is to your own personal interpretation of the higher power you must turn for answers and for the strength to endure. There is an old Muslim saying: "Allah has all the answers, provided one knows the questions." A belief system in a higher power, which I choose to refer to simply as God, is vital. The first step to healing from grief is through faith—in God and in the realization that the soul is immortal.

I use the term *the Other Side* for this dimension to which our spirit transfers. The name for the Other Side varies depending upon one's faith: Heaven, the Afterlife, Nirvana, Paradise, the House of the Lord, Celestial Kingdom, and Tian, to name just a few. Religions have different opinions as to what that other realm is like and where it is, yet they all agree that it exists and that physical death is not the end.

Traditional religions have tended to depict the Other Side as a distant and aloof realm that is only reachable through a particular religion's dogma and clerics. Thankfully, with the advent of interfaith dialog, this appears to be changing. It is finally becoming accepted that the Other Side is accessible to everyone, not just a select group who follow a particular creed.

Ever since I was a child, I have heard that God works in mysterious ways. It doesn't matter whether you are a person here in the material world or a spirit on the Other Side; you may have the privilege and the responsibility to act as an instrument of God's will and healing power. For those in the material world, this responsibility may be difficult and must be approached with reverence and humility.

For spirits, their role may be to become positive influences in our lives. They are aware of what is happening with us physically, emotionally, mentally, and spiritually. Spirits can see and feel our pain, and they will reach out to us in order to help us in many ways. Essentially, spirits come to the rescue of the bereaved to comfort, teach, reassure, resolve issues, and, most importantly, to love.

We are all capable of being contacted by spirits. It doesn't take a special gift to sense the presence of a deceased loved one or receive a message from that spirit. It is also a tremendous source of resolve and healing. It helps to know a loved one who has passed continues to exist, to love, and to be aware of what is going on in our lives. This soothes our need to know a loved one is happy on the Other Side.

How often do people in this life search out an opportunity to say "I'm sorry" or "I love you" to loved ones and family members? Coping with death often motivates people to evaluate their past behavior. One of the easiest ways to avoid having regrets such as this is to simply say "I love you." Whenever you end a conversation with someone you love, even if you are upset or angry, say "I love you." You can never know if that is the last thing you ever will say to that person. Wouldn't you rather have your last words with someone you love be kind and loving than heated and angry?

All too often, people bypass this simple opportunity, and it leaves them full of regret for not sharing their most important thoughts with their loved ones while they still could. It is good to know they don't have to give up hope: through spirit contact, it is still possible to resolve regrets with loved ones on the Other Side.

Spirits also hope to resolve regrets and issues with people in the material world, although spirits have the advantage of being able to perceive things from a fresh perspective. It is as if they "can see clearly now the rain is gone." Free of the pain, suffering, emotional upset, and tribulations of life, a spirit can perceive more clearly what he or she did while in the material world and how it might be remedied from the Other Side.

My life's mission is to use my training as an attorney and my gift of spirit communication as a medium to help people cope with the crushing effects of grief. By making contact with a spirit on the Other Side, one's faith that the soul continues on after physical death can be validated. Spirit contact is not only possible, it is much more common and accessible than is generally accepted.

THROUGH MEDIUMSHIP, MY perspective on death changed. For me, mediumship was a gift of healing from God. A gift from God must not be questioned or doubted, only accepted, embraced, and used selflessly in the service of others. I am honored that this ability runs in my family and privileged that I am able to share this gift.

Spirit contact is a truly amazing thing to experience. I've conducted thousands of readings for people, connecting them with loved ones on the Other Side, and the messages of love and healing from the afterlife never cease to amaze me. However, making contact with the Other Side is just a part of the healing process. The journey through grief is like walking from Florida to California. Spirit contact through a medium might get you to Georgia; the rest of the journey is up to you.

The first step in healing is faith in God and belief in the immortality of the soul: a firm conviction and belief that when we die, we continue to exist. Faith brings comfort by removing the fear that nonexistence is what awaits us when we die. The words of my mother, Jeannie Anthony, explain it best:

"Death is not the end. Death is not sad for the one who passed. It is only sad for those who remain behind. To heal from the sadness of death, you must have faith in the knowledge that one day you will be reunited with those you love on the Other Side, in the Light of the Holy Spirit and in the love that is God."

Doubt Is Part
of the Journey

*M*y close friend Katharine is the quintessential classy, sophisticated Man-
hattan business executive. She likes to joke that
she has my phone number on "psychic speed
dial." During one of our telephone conversations,
Katharine confided that she began to doubt her
faith in God after the death of someone she loved.
She told me she sought the counsel of her rabbi,
who responded, "How can you have faith without
doubt?"

Faith in God and in an afterlife is especially difficult during times of loss. It is easy to think you have lost a loved one when that person's physical body ceases to function. But faith teaches us we never lose anyone—that people really don't die. The spirit, the personality, and the unique expression of the sum of a person lives on beyond physical life. Sometimes you just need a spirit to help you fully understand this.

People often come to me for readings, not only to make contact with a deceased loved one but also for validation of their belief system. But even mediums have doubts during times of loss; crises of faith happen to everyone. This hit home when James, my friend and fellow medium, called me the day after his mother had died of cancer.

"Mark, is it all true?" he asked.

"Go on, James," I responded, knowing he needed to talk.

"I just can't help thinking that, well, maybe it isn't true. Maybe there is nothing after this life." It was clear he was reeling from the stark, cold reality that his mother had just died.

"Are you saying that you're having a crisis of faith?" I asked.

"Yeah, I guess I am," James said, fighting tears and straining to maintain his composure.

"Of all people, you should know that we go on after the body ceases to function." I tried to explain. "Once our body stops working, our spirit is freed and ascends to the Other Side. I know you understand this, James. I've seen you do dozens of readings for people."

"I know; I'm just scared," James said, "and I don't know what to think or what to feel. It is all so surreal. I can't seem to focus on anything. It's like I'm on the outside of my body, looking at myself just going through the motions. I'm walking through a nightmare, and I just want to wake up and not be in so much pain. I feel so guilty for having these thoughts and thinking maybe I'll never hear from her again."

"Many spiritual people have these crises of faith. You are a devout Catholic, right?" I asked.

"I don't feel like much of one now," he almost whispered.

"That may be, but don't be so hard on yourself," I said. "Even Mother Teresa, who cared for so many sick and dying people, is reputed to have gone through a period when even she wondered if God existed at all."

"Come to think of it," James responded, "on the cross, Jesus cried out, 'My God, my God, why have you forsaken me?'"

"I never thought of it that way," I replied. "So don't feel bad because you are having doubts. You're in good company."

"Mark, you have so much faith. You make it seem so simple to just believe. I appreciate that," James said graciously.

"Trust me, it wasn't easy—it's been a long road getting here," I replied.

STRENGTH OF FAITH isn't something that comes easily. It can take a lifetime. I certainly didn't do it alone; I had a lot of help, both from this side of existence and from the Other

Side. Coming from a psychic family definitely helped. As a Catholic, I was taught that faith is believing and yet not seeing. Maybe mediums have an unfair advantage since we not only believe, we also see.

Looking back on my childhood, I can only say it was a privilege to be raised by a psychic mother. My siblings and I didn't think she was different or weird, because that's just how Mom was, and it seemed normal to us.

I might come home from school to find Mom with an enlightened expression on her face. "I saw a spirit today," she'd say.

"That's cool, Mom. Do we have any peanut butter?"

"Yes, honey, it's over there."

As we got older, we learned not everyone's mom had the talents of our mother. She seemed to know things about us: where we'd been, what we'd been up to, and who we'd been with.

This phenomenon was not unusual. Psychic ability has existed in my family for at least a century. My mother's family emigrated from Italy and settled in Newark, New Jersey. They were devout Catholics and openly embraced their psychic abilities, which they referred to as "second sight." One of the best stories about how a spirit helped resolve doubts about the existence of an afterlife involves my maternal grandfather, Rocco Aurena. My mother was extremely close to her father. She always said he was gentle, compassionate, and loving.

Rocco Aurena found his faith in the waters of the Mediterranean. During World War I, while serving in the Italian

Navy, Rocco's ship was torpedoed by a German U-boat. Nearly 100 men went down with the ship. For two days, Rocco watched in horror as his shipmates drowned or were devoured by sharks. Desperately, he clung to a piece of wreckage and prayed to God for deliverance. On the third day, his prayers were answered, and he was rescued. He was one of only three survivors.

After that experience, Rocco became a deeply religious man. He taught my mother that, no matter what, you must believe in God and you must believe in Heaven. "God is always listening, Jeannie," he often told her.

Sadly, Rocco then *lost* his faith in November 1963 when his mother-in-law, my great-grandmother and the matriarch of the family, Giovanna Senna, died. Giovanna, a devout Catholic, believed wholeheartedly in God. She was also a great psychic and medium who was known in the Italian community as "the woman who knew things." Giovanna treated Rocco as a son, and he loved her like a mother. While the entire family was emotionally devastated by the passing of Giovanna, it was Rocco Aurena who seemed the most affected.

As the casket was lowered into the ground at the graveside service for Giovanna, my mother, Jeannie, wept in her father's arms.

"Daddy," Jeannie sobbed, "will we see her again? Will we see her in Heaven?"

Nothing prepared her for Rocco's response. "No," he replied coldly. "There is nothing. There is no God. It is all lies. When you die, you die and crumble into dust."

Shocked at his response, Jeannie stared at her father. "How can you say such a thing?"

As he stared at Giovanna's grave, he shook his head and repeated, "There's nothing."

"But you were always so pious and religious. You prayed. You believed in God." Jeannie was horrified.

Unbeknownst to the family, Rocco was slowly dying of cancer. The excruciating pain transformed this loving, gentle man into one driven by fear, anger, doubt, and resentment.

NOT LONG AFTER Giovanna's death, my family moved to Florida from New Jersey. One Sunday morning, on December 13, 1964, something remarkable happened.

Everyone was sleeping. Precisely at 7 AM, my mother sat up in bed, wide awake. Startled by her sudden movement, my father opened his eyes. He was amazed by the look of astonishment on Jeannie's face. She had awakened to see her father, Rocco Aurena, standing in the doorway of her bedroom.

"Daddy!" Jeannie gasped. "What are you doing here?"

Rocco stood before her, not as an old man dying of cancer but as her handsome and healthy father. He looked as youthful as he had in his early twenties. Jeannie said she recognized his hazel eyes and his charming, dimpled smile. He was dressed in a red flannel shirt and blue slacks, and he was wearing his favorite fedora.

Jeannie heard him say in a familiar voice, "There is something beyond this life, and it is wonderful!"

He smiled again and tipped his hat—something he always did before he left a room—and vanished.

Jeannie, knowing innately that it was true, cried out, "Daddy's dead!"

My father tried to reassure her. But based on her expression, Earl knew Jeannie had witnessed something otherworldly.

Jeannie leapt from her bed and phoned her family; no answer. She expected the worst. Two hours later, her brother, my uncle Joey, called to say my grandfather, Rocco Aurena, had died at 7 AM.

Barely a year before, while still living in the material world, Rocco had told Jeannie that nothing existed beyond this life. But once he crossed over, his spirit came to the rescue to show her there *is* an afterlife: "There is something beyond this life, and it is wonderful!" Rocco Aurena came to his daughter at the moment of his physical death to say he'd been completely wrong—and to say goodbye.

Although she'd always been psychically inclined and had even seen and felt the presence of spirits around her, this experience was different. She had seen her father standing in her bedroom doorway as clearly as if he were alive. She had heard his voice.

This visitation was a life-changing event for my mother. It solidified her firm belief in God and in the afterlife. She never doubted her psychic and mediumistic abilities again.

The story of Rocco's spiritual influence did not end that day in 1964. Spirits have a way of continuing to make their presence felt, although it may take a lifetime of reflection before the true meaning of an event involving spirit contact is fully understood.

ROCCO AURENA HAD ten grandchildren. One of them happens to look exactly like Rocco; I am that grandchild.

In the 1980s, I attended law school at Mercer University in Macon, Georgia. First-semester exams had just ended, and I planned to drive back to Florida on the following day to spend winter break with my family.

For no reason I can explain, I perceived a voice directing me, "You must go home now." Although I was exhausted from exams, I packed up my clothes, jumped in my van, and headed to Florida a day early.

Two months earlier, at the law school Halloween party, I had gone as Indiana Jones, wearing a fedora as part of the costume. I wanted to show it off to my parents, so I wore it on the drive home. It was a cold, windy night, and to keep warm, I was wearing a red flannel shirt and blue jeans. Just before seven o'clock in the evening, I pulled into the driveway of my parents' house. As I opened the front door, a breeze ominously rushed into the living room with me. Before I could say "Surprise, I'm home!" my mother screamed and ran out of the room. *That was pretty odd*, I thought. "Dad, what's up with Mom?"

Looking up from his newspaper, my father said, "Who knows? You know how your mother is."

I went to my room to unpack, and my mother eventually joined me. A tear ran down her cheek. In barely a whisper, she said, "I'm sorry I screamed. But when you walked in the door wearing that fedora, blue jeans, and red flannel shirt, you looked exactly like my father did when he appeared to me at the moment of his death. I feel in some way he came back to me again. He died twenty years ago today."

It was December 13, 1984.

I HAVE OFTEN heard about people being "born again" by a life-changing spiritual experience. While I do not yet consider myself "born again" in the sense that religious people do, I did have a life-changing spiritual experience at a Catholic church in Melbourne, Florida. A woman named Sofia was conducting a healing service one evening in 1999. It sounded interesting, so I thought I'd go.

This was a point in my life when I was wavering in my faith. In fact, I was plagued with doubt regarding the existence of God. I believed in God, at least in the theoretical sense. I'd been raised to believe in God, but now I was questioning that belief. Maybe years of practicing law had made me skeptical and cynical. At the time, I found that whenever

I spoke about God, I would equivocate or say something like, "When you die, you go to Heaven—that is, if Heaven exists." Other times, I would question, "If there is a God, does God really care about us?" Now that I look back on this, I find it bizarre that, after being raised by psychic parents, having psychically inclined siblings, and being exposed to all of the spirituality that was around me on a daily basis, I could ever question the existence of God. Perhaps I had just come to a state of spiritual stagnation—that was, until I met Sofia.

From what I understand, the power of the Holy Spirit flows through Sofia. Sofia herself says, "It is not *I* who heal people, it is the power of *God,* who works through me." I was amazed during the service at how engaging her words were, yet I sat there, self-absorbed in my own problems.

Sofia called forth all those who were suffering from illnesses. She then said, "Illness comes in many forms. It is not always physical. There is someone who is having a struggle with his faith."

I was stunned as I realized she was looking directly at me. Obviously this message was meant for me. I stood and approached Sofia. I looked at several of the people around me who had severe physical problems. I was just having a crisis of faith. I was embarrassed. Nonetheless, I silently asked God, "Why is this happening to me?"

I heard a serene voice that simply said, "Stop denying me."

I was stunned. This was an intense clairaudient experience, which means I heard the voice from within. The strange part was that it was not the voice I hear in my head when I think. It spoke concisely, with conviction and authority, yet it was serene. It said everything in those few words, for I realized then that, despite my doubts, I *did* believe in God. At the same moment, I recognized the fact that I had been wavering in that belief for years. I had gone through the motions but didn't feel the connection to God in my heart. Now I did.

From that point on, everything changed. I did not run out to become an evangelist or join an extremist religious organization, and I did not regularly attend Catholic church. Instead of becoming religious, I became spiritual. Being spiritual means having a connection to God based on personal experience rather than faith in God based on organized religion, dogma, procedure, or a set of rules. It is a "knowing" that God exists and a connection to God. Being spiritual does not mean you cannot or should not be part of a religion, just that the personal connection with God transcends an organization created by humans. Deep within me, I could acknowledge with certainty what I'd always known: God exists.

DESPITE THIS AFFIRMATION of faith, I experienced another crisis when my mother passed some years later.

Two days after her death, I wondered, *Where is she? Did Mom just crumble into dust? Did she just cease to exist?*

I panicked as an adrenalin rush of fear surged through me.

Once again, doubt overcame me. I thought, *Maybe there is no God.*

I wondered, *Is everything I've learned about death and the after-life just a fairy tale designed to make us feel better about things over which we have no control? Are religions just a way to manipulate and control people? Is God just a delay concept to help the human mind explain the unexplainable?*

All of these thoughts raced through my head. Fear and doubt flooded my heart. If hell existed on earth, I was in it. I felt my faith drain from me. I lay on my bed and passed out from exhaustion around midnight.

At four in the morning, I lurched awake and sat up in bed. I heard the voice. I recognized it from years before. Again, the voice spoke to me with such serenity: "In dying, we are born to eternal life." This message meant a lot to me, since it is from the last line of the Prayer of Saint Francis. Of course, when someone dies, it is natural to pray a lot, and this is a popular prayer, but I heard it in "the voice." This was another clairaudient message sent to me. I was in need of help from God—and my prayer was answered. Suddenly, I felt renewed. My fear subsided, and my faith returned. Maybe my faith never was gone, but I needed a metaphorical slap in the face to snap out of my fears.

The next day, I explained to my friend Joe what had happened. He is a very spiritual person and a fundamentalist Christian. I was comfortable talking about my experience with him. I told Joe about how I felt my faith drain from me in my fear—and I told him about the voice.

He asked, "Didn't you tell me about that voice once before, years ago?"

Surprised he had remembered that story, I answered yes.

"Well," Joe continued, "didn't it occur to you that God told you that so you would have faith to prepare you for what you are going through now? God may have told you years ago, but time isn't limiting to God."

"That is true," I responded.

"God is all-knowing and all-seeing," Joe said. "I may not see spirits or hear the voice of God, but I still believe. The book of Job teaches us that it is easy to believe in God when everything is going well. It is in the trying times that finding your faith is the challenge."

"Yes, that's true, too," I admitted.

"You received a message from God. How many people must endure grief without a confirmation from Heaven?" he asked.

"I'm sure that's the case for most people," I replied.

"You have to have faith, Mark," Joe told me. "Faith is believing and yet not seeing. You have to have faith in God to carry you through this time of darkness. We may abandon God, but God *never* abandons us."

I was amazed at how concisely he put everything into perspective for me. Suddenly, my doubts and fears were overcome by my faith. I saw clearly that God is *the* multidimensional being and a vast intelligence transcending all time, space, and distance. God is the source of all life, light, love, and understanding. God pervades every living cell. The experiences of all living things are connected to God.

Even when negative events occur, like the death of a loved one, this is part of God's experience, too. How we react to these events is part of our life plan and the lessons that come with it. Without these challenges, we would not progress or learn. Our interactions with others and our efforts to overcome our pain teach us that God never abandons us, because we are part of God. We are all connected.

SUE SHARED WITH me how faith had brought the color back into her life. Sue has a bright, bubbly personality and is always upbeat and cheerful. It is hard to imagine Sue ever having a bad day. However, after I met Sue, I kept sensing a strong feminine spiritual presence around her. Finally one day, while visiting her home, I said, "Sue, this may sound odd, but there's a spirit around you."

"Mark, you're a medium; seeing spirits is what you do. Why is that so odd?" Sue asked with a smile.

"That's just it," I replied. "This spirit, well, looks exactly like you, except her hair isn't as long as yours."

Sue stopped and turned to me. Although her mouth was smiling, her eyes were not. She walked to the kitchen and opened a drawer. "Let me show you something." She took a photograph from the drawer and handed it to me.

The yellowed photo looked at least twenty-five years old. It depicted two women in their twenties—Sue and a woman who looked exactly like her.

"That's me with my identical twin sister. I was named SueAnn and she was named LouAnn. We were the type of identical twins who always experienced what the other one was feeling. Lou and I could communicate without even talking. If one of us got sick, the other had the symptoms without having the illness—we were that connected. We were a part of each other," Sue explained. "Then one night, Lou was killed by a drunk driver in a collision on the causeway."

"I'm so sorry," I responded.

"I only lived a few miles from the scene. The police called me to identify her body. That was the worst thing I've ever had to do."

"That must've been horrible," I told her.

"You can't even imagine what that was like for me. You should've seen the reaction of the police when I walked into the morgue. They didn't know Lou and I were identical twins. One of the cops was on his way out of the morgue as I was coming in. He really flipped out when he saw me."

I remained silent, knowing there was more she needed to share.

"I always thought how lucky I was to have an identical twin, except when she was killed. It was like half of me died— the half I could never get back. My life became so bleak. I couldn't see color for a year after she died. All the joy in my life was gone. I didn't notice flowers; I couldn't even hear birds sing. Everything turned gray. I was so overcome with depression and so angry."

"No one can blame you for that," I said.

"I was angry at that drunk who killed her. I was angry at the court system. The guy who killed my sister didn't even go to prison. He only got a year of work release. I've heard since then he's been arrested three more times for drunk driving."

"Our justice system is often a failure," I said.

"Most of all, I was angry at God. I doubted if God even existed. How could a loving God do this to Lou? She never hurt anybody. I doubted everything I was ever taught in church. I stopped believing in anything beyond the pain I felt. Without Lou, I started to feel there was no point in living anymore."

"Something happened to change that, didn't it?" I asked.

"Yes, but it took a long time. Going to church became meaningless for me. Even so, I still prayed every day for an answer. Then, somehow, I just felt that Lou still existed as a spirit. Even though death separated us, we were still connected. I didn't see or hear her—it was more of an understanding. Even though I felt I couldn't live without her, I learned I had to. It dawned on me that everything happens for a reason, no matter how painful. I no longer doubted there was a life beyond this one. My faith in God saved my life, because I came to believe there is an afterlife."

"Finding faith is difficult. Your journey was especially painful," I commented.

"I was always taught faith is believing and yet not seeing," Sue explained.

"I agree with that," I replied, remembering that my friend Joe had told me the same thing.

"But there's more to it than that. When you believe, you begin to see."

"What do you mean?" I asked.

"One morning, I felt a need to watch the sun rise over the ocean, so I walked to the beach before dawn. As the sun rose on the horizon, it struck me how beautiful the silvery-green ocean was. Then I saw how bright orange the sun was, and that the sky was filled with every shade of pink, yellow, and blue. It was at that moment I realized I'd overcome my doubts. I could see color again!"

IT'S OKAY WHEN we doubt our faith in God, because this is part of our material-world experience. Doubt occurs in the struggle to find faith and is often present in the journey through grief. When we overcome our doubts by faith, we are made stronger. Faith is an understanding that God exists and that everything that happens to us is touched by God. When we accept that we are eternal beings having a temporary material-world existence, our perspective on death changes. We can find comfort in the knowledge that the soul is immortal.

Truly, there can be no faith without doubt. When we are adrift in the sea of doubt, clinging to the wreckage of fear, we must realize that a crisis of faith during a time of loss is only natural. Overcoming doubt is one of life's great spiritual tests. Healing begins when we realize that doubts are but fleeting fears that can be washed away by faith in God and belief in the reality of the afterlife.

3

Finding the Right Path
Through Grief

*W*inston Churchill once remarked, "If you're going through hell, keep going." Grief is hell on earth, and finding the right path through it is essential to the healing process. Spirits can help us with this journey, yet choosing the appropriate means of coping is ultimately up to us.

We cannot change the fact that someone we love has died. For those who remain behind, the death of a loved one is a life-altering event. Even in situations where death is expected, no one is truly prepared for the gravity of the changes that occur. Often these changes are painful, lonely, difficult—and terrifying. The consequences may include depression or financial ruin. It is hell. Yet there are many different ways to cope with grief. Accepting the reality of the situation and finding the right personal path will get you through this hell and lead to important lessons.

IN MY WORK as an attorney and as a medium, I encounter a lot of people coping with the death of loved ones. Sometimes, a coping strategy is simply doing something to positively influence those around you. Many people find volunteer work a soothing consolation when they are enduring the grieving process. In those cases, the path through grief becomes a motivating force for goodness.

One woman I was privileged to meet, a retired concert pianist, found herself widowed after fifty-two years of marriage. Instead of sitting home alone in a sea of self-pity, she pushed herself to be active, to go to a senior citizen retirement community and play the piano. Her amazing talent not only entertained the seniors there, it gave them the opportunity to give back: they welcomed her as a friend. Many were also widowed and could listen with a sympathetic ear when she talked about her pain. This new venue may not have been Carnegie Hall (where she had once performed), but never before had she felt so much satisfaction from playing piano.

Although she never stopped missing her beloved husband, she had found a creative means of moving through her grief.

A young man named Nick had suffered greatly in the span of just two years when three of his family members died. He sought grief counseling at a local church. After nearly a year in the group, he wanted to become a counselor himself. Nick completed the training, and he now facilitates a grief counseling group.

In my mediumship development classes, many people are drawn to the training because they are seeking answers. Having lost loved ones, they try to develop mediumship ability to make contact. Others, like Benjamin, come to expand their own spiritual understanding.

Benjamin was an affable seventy-nine-year-old gentleman. He missed his late wife terribly. Although he never quite got over her passing, he'd begun to date other women. Connecting with his psychic abilities brought him comfort in the realization that his wife's death was not the end of her but rather her transformation to another level of existence. For Benjamin, this understanding was the path to inner peace.

These are just a few examples of positive responses to the misery inflicted by death. I have tremendous respect for the people who cope in these ways. They could have collapsed under the weight of grief or taken on a victim identity, but instead they decided to turn their sorrow into something inspired by love and to help other suffering people.

That is why it is important to reach out to those who love you—and to seek help. Help is available, but it is up to you to ask for it. If you are suffering excessively with grief, perhaps grief counseling may be the appropriate approach. Many churches offer grief share groups and counseling. Some people prefer a secular form of counseling; others may seek the assistance of a doctor and take prescribed medication for depression. Sometimes all that is needed is the listening ear of a friend or another compassionate person who has gone through loss. While we may all grieve in our own way, grieving people have a lot in common. It helps to learn how others manage their suffering—and how they were able to get through it.

Spirits on the Other Side know and feel the pain of the survivors. They want to help and be a positive influence in our lives. While we may mourn the loss of a loved one, I've yet to encounter a spirit who regretted being on the Other Side. The spirits I connect with usually seem so happy, and they want their loved ones in the material world to know this.

THERE ARE MANY pitfalls when one cannot accept the reality of a death. Unresolved, prolonged grief can become an obsession or lead to obsessive behaviors that are unhealthy and counterproductive. Some people become so mired in their grief that it consumes their lives and outlooks. The grief can take on a life of its own and actually become one's life. I saw this firsthand when I met Tonya.

Tonya had come to me for a reading in order to connect with her deceased son. She was pleased with the reading and invited me to speak at a support group for parents who have lost children. She told me she thought I might be able to help some of the people there. I was honored and accepted her invitation.

Before I was permitted to speak at the support group, everyone in the room explained, in graphic detail, how his or her child had died. For two hours, each of these people relived the experience, and most of the members of the group reinforced the sadness. Many explained how they hated Halloween because they couldn't bear to see other children having fun. Another woman said she hated Christmas and other holidays because they reminded her of her son. The group agreed it was okay to hate holidays and to avoid them altogether.

Without a doubt, the death of a child is the worst pain imaginable. However, many people in this group had been there for more than five years. Instead of sharing ways to cope and how to work to get better, they relived the deaths of their children—and concluded the meetings without any resolution, hope, or direction toward healing. When it came time for me to speak, I was informed by the group's facilitator that I only had three minutes. I was taken aback; most of my presentations last an hour. It appeared many of the group members were annoyed that a guest speaker—an intruder— had been invited.

There was no healing taking place in this group. Other grief support groups I had attended were designed to assist people in accepting the death, enduring the grieving process, and embracing their current life as the new normal. Without realizing it, this group appeared to encourage an unending circle of grief designed to sustain the pain.

In an unending circle of grief, the bereaved never progress. The unconscious intent is to hold on to the sorrow and to validate the grief by characterizing it as more profound than anyone else's. Statements such as "See how much I suffer" or "If you knew what I'd been through" or "No one hurts like I do" identify those who cannot move on. I don't for one second downplay their pain, but, while grief makes us all victims, there may come a time when one goes from being victimized by it to volunteering to be its victim. This is not healthy.

Hank, one of the gentlemen in the group, captured my attention. He told the group that two years earlier, his twenty-two-year-old son had committed suicide. "I thought he was stronger than that," he said. "I'm so disappointed and angry at him. I'm disgusted to think he was so weak. It's not like his death was an accident. At least your kids didn't kill themselves."

Hank's comments definitely offended some of the other group members. Nevertheless, while he was speaking, I perceived the spirit of his son next to him. The young man's spirit started showing me shared memories he had with his father. I could see Hank taking his son to Little League and the two of them laughing and playing baseball together. The son was trying to console his father and communicate that his suicide was the result of depression. He hadn't been thinking clearly when he had decided to commit suicide, because his depression had consumed him. The son didn't realize how much pain would be caused by his death, and he wanted to apologize to his father.

"Excuse me, sir," I said to Hank, "but if it isn't intruding, you may wish to consider—"

"I'm not talking to *you!*" Hank said loudly as he stood up and practically ran out of the room, slamming the door behind him.

Tonya winked at me and whispered, "Don't feel bad about that. We hear the same thing every month. It's like he's stuck in quicksand. He never wants to forgive his son, poor man."

Clearly, Hank was not ready for spirit contact with his son. I understood this and didn't take it personally. Spirit contact may not be for everyone, and as a medium, I must respect their feelings. However, healing *is* for everyone, and there comes a time when you must decide to heal and move forward with your life.

Despite Hank's outburst, some of the group members were interested in spirit contact. They didn't want to volunteer to be victims of grief. They wanted to heal and realized that this support group was not helping them do that. After the meeting, I spoke to them about various coping techniques, suggested some books, and referred them to some grief counselors and other support groups. Although I knew I'd gotten through to a few of them, when I left, I prayed I'd have the opportunity to do more.

My prayers were answered the next week when a number of the group members contacted me for readings. It was my privilege to oblige, and from the feedback I received, the readings were beneficial to them.

GRIEF CAN BE so overwhelming and powerful that sometimes you will do anything to just not hurt anymore. As a criminal defense attorney, I'm well acquainted with people who have drug and alcohol problems. Addictions arise in many people who improperly deal with grief. Chain smoking, drinking to excess, and drug usage are common self-destructive behaviors. Addiction is a "cover behavior," the result of practicing pain aversion instead of processing and working through grief to find the life lessons.

Tim was a twenty-seven-year-old surfing instructor who had come to see me in my capacity as a criminal defense attorney. He explained that he had a prior drunk driving charge and had recently been arrested for possession of marijuana. He fidgeted in his chair, and I could see he was extremely nervous. As we talked, I felt a strong maternal spiritual presence connected with Tim begin to take form on his right side.

I began to focus on the spirit without realizing that I had all but tuned out Tim, who was talking about his anxiety disorder and how he drank and smoked marijuana to calm down. All of a sudden, he stopped talking and looked over his right shoulder, then back to me.

"What're you looking at?" he asked abruptly.

This client conference now became awkward. He was in my office for his criminal problems, not for a reading. I wasn't sure how to answer, but before I could, he broke the silence.

"You see things other people don't, don't you?" Tim asked, glancing nervously over his right shoulder again. "What do you see?"

It began to dawn on me that, on some level, Tim was aware of the presence of spirits. The rough part was that he didn't understand his own mediumistic ability. His lack of understanding seemed to compound his overall anxiety.

"Tim," I said calmly, going back into lawyer mode, "all of your arrests seem to have happened since April of last year. Before that, you had a clean record, right?"

"Yeah," he said, again glancing suspiciously over his right shoulder.

Going out on a limb, I decided to take a chance and asked, "Did someone close to you die before April of last year?"

Tim's eyes clouded with tears. "My mom did, and I miss her so much. Right after she died, I couldn't handle it. I started drinking a lot and smoking weed. She died in March, and then a month later, I got busted for drunk driving. She was the only family I had; I'm so alone without her. She always knew what to do. Without her, it's like I'm out of control."

"Does getting drunk and high help you cope with her passing?" I asked.

"Not really, it's just that I can't handle it. It hurts so much. I don't know where to turn. You know the surfer crowd— they're all tough guys who don't want to listen to me whine about my mom's death. I have no one to talk to," he confided. Tears rolled down his cheeks.

"Tough guys hurt, too, when someone they love dies. Don't be so hard on your friends. One thing, though, is clear: self-medicating isn't doing you any good. It's getting you into trouble." I continued, "Your mother doesn't want you getting drunk and stoned all the time."

"What do you mean?" he asked, looking shaken.

"I mean, if your mother were here in this room, she would say that she wants you to stop drinking and getting high," I said, conveying to him the message from the Other Side.

"Yeah, she'd be totally disappointed in me," Tim said as he looked down.

"Then it is time to make your mom proud of you again," I said, handing him a tissue. "She wants you to get help coping with this. I'd also like to recommend an addiction counselor who has some expertise in grief counseling. Would you be interested in that?"

"You really think my mom knows what is going on with me?" Tim asked, regaining his composure.

"I'm sure of it," I told him.

"All of this drama is wearing me out. You talk like she's here now; is she?" he asked, glancing over his shoulder again.

"Better question: do *you* feel she is around you?" I asked.

"That's the freaky part; I do," he replied, confirming my suspicion that he was sensitive to the presence of spirits.

"Do you find that comforting?" I asked.

"Yeah, I do—and no, I don't. It's like she is watching over me, except she's not too happy with what she sees," he said mournfully.

"Suffice it to say you aren't dealing with her death properly. You need a new direction—one that doesn't involve intoxication. Take things one step at a time. Let me deal with your legal problems. Your job is to go to counseling and get sober," I told him.

Tim made a lot of progress in counseling and actually stayed sober. He was referred to a doctor, who put him on an anti-anxiety drug. Although he never did come for a reading, the last time I heard from him, he was doing well on his own.

OTHER EVERYDAY BEHAVIORS that may appear normal on the surface can be just as destructive as drug or alcohol addiction, such as plunging into a new relationship as a distraction from the death of a loved one. Diving into a feel-good relationship soon after the death of a loved one is not the proper path through grief. Relationships take time to cultivate, and meteoric romances all too often become meteorites that crash and burn. These relationships can also be dangerous, because they may allow bereaved individuals to become targets for manipulative personalities.

Melinda missed Jerome, her husband of thirty-five years, immensely. Jerome had died of cancer and, due to his estate planning, Melinda was left with a modest income for the rest of her life—that is, until Frederick showed up.

Melinda lived in a small house in a middle-class neighborhood. Barely two months after Jerome's death, she was in her front yard pulling weeds.

"I can help you do that," said a male voice from behind her.

Melinda turned around and looked up. Standing there was a good-looking twenty-seven-year-old man with a disarming smile. "My name's Frederick. I'm looking for some work. I'm between jobs."

She agreed to give him yardwork and handyman jobs around the house. As they got to know one another, Melinda was taken with the younger man's charm. He seemed to hang on to her every word. He always looked her in the eyes when he spoke. He was sweet and kind to her. He made her laugh. He told Melinda that he was in the process of looking for a new place to live. Within days, Frederick had moved into Melinda's house.

Frederick always knew just what to say to make Melinda feel attractive. When Melinda asked why a young man would be interested in a woman of sixty-two, Frederick replied, "Age is just a number. When I look at you, I see a vibrant young woman." Of course, this is exactly what a bereaved widow wants to hear. Melinda wanted to feel young and attractive again.

I was representing Melinda in a civil matter and noticed she started bringing Frederick with her to my office. Although charming, he was extremely domineering and talked over her and for her. He tried to ingratiate himself to me, but he seemed so insincere. I had a bad feeling about him.

As a psychic, when I meet someone, I usually pick up on their feelings or get some impressions or images from them. While I don't try to read them, I believe this is a natural side effect of being psychic. The strange thing about Frederick was that I never felt any emotion from him; he felt like an empty shell. Then one day when Melinda brought him to my office, I understood why.

During the course of the client conference, Melinda excused herself to go to the ladies' room. When she left the room, Frederick leaned forward. "You don't like me, do you?" he asked in a whisper. His seemingly cheerful disposition had transformed into something sinister. Finally, I felt an emotion emanating from him: icy malevolence.

"Is there something you're doing to Melinda that you should feel guilty about?" I asked.

"I don't do guilt," he sneered. "Besides, she'll never listen to anything bad about me, so don't even try."

He switched to an intimidation tactic by staring directly into my eyes and not blinking, trying to get me to blink or look away first. I met the challenge and continued staring back while visualizing a wall of white light between us, protecting me. After some moments, he broke off eye contact and looked away.

"You're out of your league, Frederick. Your little games don't work on me," I informed him.

He glared back at me with an expression of rage. At that moment, Melinda returned, and Frederick resumed his puppy-dog personality, gazing at her with feigned love.

Unfortunately, my suspicions were confirmed: Frederick was a sociopath. I've dealt with several sociopaths in my many years of experience as a prosecutor and a criminal defense attorney. They are, in my opinion, the dark energies who walk among us. They are incapable of the emotion of love, and they are completely amoral. Their lack of love may have something to do with the reason I can't read them. Psychic and mediumistic abilities are based in love. Sociopaths are devoid of love, immersing themselves in pools of negative energy. This gives a psychic nothing to read.

These types of people are especially dangerous to the bereaved. Sociopaths view themselves as the predators and everyone else as prey. Nothing matters to sociopaths except their own selfish desires. Since the bereaved are perfect victims and sociopaths are perfect predators, it is a tragic match.

Sociopaths like Frederick can be charming and endearing. They often seek out bereaved people who are desperately lonely. As pathological liars, sociopaths effortlessly tell a person what that person wants to hear—but, in a flash, can change their tone and personality.

Frederick had a pattern of relationships with widows. He accomplished this by searching the obituary column of the local newspaper to identify the recently widowed. Since an obituary lists survivors' names, a sociopath knows how many family members he has to contend with, and the fewer, the better. Given Melinda's age and that her son lived out of state, she was perfect for his purposes.

To most people, the idea of taking advantage of someone suffering from the loss of a loved one is reprehensible. To a sociopath, it is all in a day's work. In Melinda's case, Frederick was not only a sociopath but also a cocaine user and a prostitute. Frederick would do anything for money to support his cocaine habit. He would sell himself to men or women. His rap sheet was long, and he was engaged in many forms of criminal activity, constantly in legal trouble and claiming to be framed.

I repeatedly tried to warn Melinda to get him out of her life, but she refused to listen. Frederick was so good at telling her lies that she wouldn't believe me when I told her about his part in the armed robbery of an elderly woman.

Eventually, Frederick siphoned all of Melinda's money and sold everything she had of value. Since Melinda could no longer afford the mortgage, the bank foreclosed on her small house. To make matters worse, Frederick had infected her with a sexually transmitted disease. Frederick used the last of her money to have her bond him out of jail. He failed to appear for court and skipped out on his bail, which cost Melinda thousands of dollars. Once Melinda was out of money, he disappeared. When I last heard from Melinda, she had to move out of state to live with her son. If not for her son, she would be homeless.

KERRI WAS AN accountant grieving the sudden loss of her mother, who had been killed in a car accident. Her parents had been married for fifty-five years, and it was a tremendous blow to the entire family. Kerri saw the toll this took on her father, Edgar.

Kerri lived close to her father's home and had a thriving practice as a CPA. To keep her father busy, Kerri offered him a job at her office doing clerical work.

Edgar tried to avoid coping with his wife's death. He wouldn't go to counseling or seek friends his own age. Instead, Edgar became obsessed with Sybil, one of Kerri's secretaries. Sybil was fifty-five years younger than Edgar.

Sybil was an attractive red-haired woman who liked to play the damsel in distress. She complained, "My husband is a lousy father. He doesn't care about our boys." Edgar willingly moved into the role of rescuer. He spent thousands of dollars on Sybil and even bought her a new car.

Kerri confronted Edgar about this inappropriate relationship. "Dad, what are you doing with Sybil? I don't want you getting personally involved with an employee."

Edgar got angry and insisted, "Mind your own business! I'm going to live my life my own way."

"Dad, I want you to stop seeing Sybil. You know there is an office policy against this. This can cause both of us a lot of problems," Kerri demanded.

"Well, that's not going to happen," Edgar replied.

"I don't understand, Dad. This woman is a stranger. You have no business giving her money. I want you to stop this silliness," Kerri implored.

"What you don't understand, Kerri, is that I'm in love with Sybil," Edgar boasted.

"Are you insane? That's ridiculous! You are old enough to be her grandfather!" Kerri was beside herself with anger.

"Well, get used to it," Edgar sneered. "She may end up leaving her husband to be with me. She might even become your new stepmother."

Kerri was mortified. She knew she needed help coping with the loss of her mother and with her father's bizarre behavior, so she decided to attend bereavement counseling. As a result, she came to realize that her father's acting out had been prompted by the loss of his beloved spouse. He feared being alone and had a frantic desire to regain his youth. In an effort to stamp out his pain, he sought a replacement.

The counselor explained to Kerri that it is common for people in long-term relationships to revert back to prior behavior patterns. Edgar saw himself as he was before he met his wife: a young marine recently discharged from the Marine Corps instead of a dignified eighty-one-year-old man.

Kerri began to have a better understanding of her father's behavior. She saw that he was living under a delusion that led him to believe every woman found him attractive. Whether it was a nurse in the hospital or a server in a restaurant who smiled at him, he was convinced they wanted him.

The reality was that he was so lonely that he was looking for any diversion to make him feel good. He sought the "high" of infatuation. He could not embrace and endure his grief, preferring instead to live in a fantasy world.

Edgar continued at a breakneck pace, pursuing Sybil every night, ignoring his doctor's advice to get more rest. Unfortunately, his age finally caught up with him. He had a stroke.

As Edgar lay in the hospital, it became clear to Kerri that Sybil did not care. She never called to see how he was doing, never visited him in the hospital, and never even sent a card. Kerri then discovered Sybil had been sleeping with more than one of the firm's clients. The final straw came when Kerri and her other employees overheard Sybil saying to a client, "At least I got a break from that old geezer. It's embarrassing being seen in public with him. And I'm so sick of Kerri. Since her mother died, she's useless as a CPA."

Finally, Kerri had had enough and confronted Sybil, who quit.

Edgar recovered from his stroke to the point where he could eventually live on his own. Counseling helped Kerri develop coping strategies, and she was able to reconcile with her father to some degree.

Kerri brought Edgar to me for a reading. Despite their smiles, I sensed tension between them. I knew nothing about them at the time, as it is my policy not to ask questions prior to conducting a reading, because I don't want it to be tainted by what I might know or feel ahead of time.

The spirit of Edgar's wife came through almost imme-diately. The spirit of his sister, mother, father, and maternal grandmother also appeared. He was thrilled to hear from his family members on the Other Side.

Toward the end of the reading, Edgar wanted to ask his wife a question.

"Go ahead," I indicated. "She's receptive."

"Do you still love me?" he asked.

"I always loved you and always will," was the reply.

"What do you think of my life now?" Edgar asked. The response was a bit awkward, and I hesitated. However, it is my job as a medium to convey the information, not specu-late on it.

"Now our children know what I had to put up with. Sometimes you are so selfish. It's like the time you bought that blue convertible without asking me first. I hated that car," was the message that came through for Edgar.

"She hated the blue convertible?" Edgar exclaimed. "I thought she liked that car!"

"You must stop thinking of yourself all the time. You've hurt your family enough. You need their forgiveness," I con-veyed, not sure what to make of his wife's message.

Edgar stared at me and then began to sob, "I'm sorry—I'm so sorry. I feel so guilty about everything I've done. No one could ever replace you. I miss you so much. It should have been me that died, not you. Can you ever forgive me?"

"I do forgive you," she replied, and then her spirit receded.

Kerri began to cry. Together, father and daughter wept. The tears they cried were tears of healing. They embraced each other lovingly.

"I'm sorry, Daddy," Kerri said. "I'm sorry for being so angry at you."

"I'm sorry, too, Kerri. I really do love you. I know I hurt your feelings," he responded.

It was clear to me that the spirit of Edgar's wife came to the rescue to help this family heal, not only from the pain associated with her passing but from the pain they had caused each other.

Kerri continued with grief counseling for a few more months, feeling it made a positive difference in her life. Edgar found a more positive way to cope with his grief. He gave himself time to grieve and to accept the reality of his wife's passing. He started dating again and met a woman his own age. When I saw them, they seemed very happy. Kerri confided that she liked this woman and told me, "She appreciates my dad for who he is—not for what's in his checkbook."

This example is not meant to discourage someone from engaging in a new relationship after a loss; quite the contrary. In the case of Edgar, he eventually met the right person. However, it is important to enter into a post-loss relationship slowly and with caution. Someone who suddenly seems so perfect might not be. Take your time. Even if the person is close in age, it's a good idea to proceed slowly and to learn about the person before making a commitment.

THE GRIEVING PROCESS is a journey we all must endure—a road everyone is forced to travel at some point in life. Accepting the fact that someone you loved has died is a painful yet crucial part of the journey. The ultimate objective is to find inner peace.

Often it's extremely difficult to find the right path through grief. The initial response to a death is shock. Once the initial shock subsides, a whole new set of fears arise. We often find that coping with grief is like being forced into the dark unknown of a vast jungle at night with no flashlight and no visible means of escape. Although you may feel lost, frightened, unprepared, overwhelmed, and doomed to failure, you can get through it and find your way out of it. You *can* survive grief.

I believe spirit contact is a powerful tool in this journey. Contact with the Other Side assists the bereaved by giving them a more positive perspective on physical death. Understanding the transition from living in the material world to living on the Other Side can lighten the burden of suffering.

While it may be beneficial for people in the material world to reach out to the Other Side, people here don't always initiate the contact. When spirits observe the suffering of a bereaved loved one, they often come to the rescue by initiating contact. Help from the Other Side is available to each of us, provided we know how to recognize it.

4

How Spirits
Contact Us

*T*hose of us living in the material world are not always the ones who take the first step in initiating communication with the Other Side. Often, it's the spirits who contact us. The important questions are whether we are open to the contact and if we will recognize it when we see it.

Contact experiences are how spirits let us know they're with us. These experiences are widespread, especially right after the death of a loved one. They manifest themselves in different forms and often involve an unexplainable event. For example, some people see the spirit of a loved one (clairvoyance), hear a message from that person (clairaudience), feel the presence of a loved one (clairsentience), smell a familiar scent associated with that person (clairscent), or, when thinking of a loved one, actually taste something associated with that person (clairgustance). Others might receive a sign from a spirit involving an unusual event that cannot be rationalized away as coincidental. A sign may include bizarre electrical phenomena. Spirits seem to be fond of using dreams as a means of contact. Many people relate finding a photo album open to a photo of their deceased loved one when no one else had access to the album. Others have reported finding an object given to them by their loved one in a place it should not have been.

My mother and I often discussed contact experiences. One conversation stands out in particular. It occurred about five years before she passed.

"What really happens when we die?" I asked her. "You always say we go on."

"Mark, I've told you how I saw my father when he appeared to me at the moment of his death," she explained. "His spirit told me, *'There is something beyond this life, and it is wonderful!'*"

"Yeah, but you're psychic. Think how many people never receive such confirmation. You see spirits, so you have real confirmation that there is an afterlife."

"Everyone can have a contact experience if they just know what to look for. I realize that for you, death is the great unknown. But it's nothing to be afraid of."

"You make it sound so easy. It's kind of spooky to me," I replied.

"Being afraid of the presence of spirits is like being afraid of the grass because it's green. It simply *is*, and you need to accept that reality."

"I appreciate that, Mom, I just don't know. I wish I could believe as strongly as you do about the afterlife."

"You're a lawyer. You like proof, so I'll prove it to you, Mark."

"How could you possibly prove it?" I asked.

"When I die, I'll contact you from the Other Side."

That was one of the greatest things about Mom—she never forgot a promise.

Five days after my mother died, I had to pick up her ashes. Since she didn't believe in cemeteries and graves, it was her wish to be cremated. This was not an easy task for me. I was still in a state of shock over her unexpected passing. I placed the container with her ashes on the back seat of my car and sat with my eyes closed. I felt I needed a few moments before starting up my car. I experienced a tingling sensation on the back of my neck, and then a flash went off in my head. Although my eyes were closed, I could see in my peripheral vision to the right, in the passenger's seat, the silhouette of my mother. I saw her profile outlined in a silver-white light. Cold chills ran through my body, followed by a warm wave of love washing over me. I felt my mother's presence and heard her voice say, "Mark, let go of the sorrow, but hold on to the love."

Immediately I realized this was another contact experience. Although I was still adrift in the dark sea of grief, this message was a beacon of hope and brought me great consolation.

I NEVER CEASE to be amazed at how creative spirits can be when they want to contact us. One of the ways spirits contact us is through signs. Signs are messages that are not always immediately apparent.

Pattie called me for a reading over the telephone. She was distraught at the passing of her mother and wanted to make contact. Her mother's spirit came through and gave Pattie several positive messages. At the end of the reading, her mother's spirit then communicated, "You'll know I'm there when you see a yellow rose."

"Okay, Mom liked roses," Pattie said, "and yellow roses were her favorites."

Pattie seemed pleased with the reading, and I was happy to have been of assistance. Two days later, I received this email message from her:

> "After I got off the phone with you, I wondered why you told me my mother said something about a yellow rose. Then I went outside where

my rose bush is, and there was a yellow rose! Mark, it was not there yesterday. In fact, there were no roses at all. And, the strange thing is, this is a pink rose bush. I was so happy. I had tears rolling down my face. Wow...I am still in shock but in a good way. Thank you so much for the work that you do. God is good."

CAMILLE ALSO RECEIVED a sign from the Other Side. She, too, had called me for a telephone reading. She wanted to connect with her late husband, Donald. His spirit came through, conveying several messages of love and reassurance for Camille. During the reading, she said, "It is wonderful to hear from him through you, Mr. Anthony, but I am wondering if he will ever contact me directly?"

"Spirits are always around us; they are connected to us through love," I answered.

"Well, I get that, but how will I know specifically that he's around me?" Camille asked.

Donald's spirit answered for me. "Dragonfly," I relayed. "Look for a dragonfly, and you'll know it's him."

"That's strange. Do you know what that means?" Camille asked.

"Not really, but it is a sign of some sort," I replied. "The message about dragonflies keeps getting repeated. He's adamant about that."

The next morning, I received a call from Camille. She was very excited.

"Mr. Anthony, you'll never believe this!" she exclaimed. "After the reading, for some reason, I felt like I needed to go to the mall."

"And?" I asked.

"When I parked my car and got out, a dragonfly kept buzzing around me," she explained, "and then I thought, *whoa!* You told me something about a dragonfly. Then I thought, no, I'm just looking for a sign. But once in the mall, I felt as if I was being guided to this jewelry store. It was so weird because I haven't been in a jewelry store since Donald died. He used to surprise me with jewelry all the time. Now all jewelry stores do is make me sad."

"Go on," I responded, wanting to hear what happened next.

"I walked in, and I couldn't believe my eyes. There was a display of jewelry by a certain artist. Dragonfly jewelry! Necklaces, rings, cameos—all with dragonflies. They were so beautiful. Then I knew I had to have been guided there by him!"

"What did you do?" I asked.

"I bought a gold dragonfly pendant, of course," she replied. "Maybe it sounds silly. But it made me feel better, like it was a surprise present from him—from Heaven."

I smiled. "I don't think finding some happiness in a message from the Other Side is silly at all," I told her.

WHILE MANY PEOPLE come to me for readings, sometimes spirits will ask me to convey a message to someone who hasn't asked for one. This creates an ethical dilemma, since a medium must never force a reading on anyone. But sometimes that is exactly what a medium may be asked to do.

One autumn day, I was visiting Cassadaga, Florida, with my friend and fellow psychic Nancy. Cassadaga is a small town not far from Daytona Beach. What distinguishes Cassadaga from other sleepy little Florida villages is that it is populated mostly by mediums and psychics. Nancy and I were there to attend a psychic fair and to listen to some of the lectures. I went as a spectator. Quite simply, I was off the psychic clock that day—or so I thought.

Nancy and I attended a lecture on the healing power of love. During the facilitator's presentation, my attention was drawn to a middle-aged woman who appeared very nervous. She stood up, said her name was Janice, and asked a question about life after death. In a pronounced Brooklyn accent, she confided, "My father recently died, and I'm so sad. My heart is breaking. I wanna know he's okay."

"Nancy," I whispered to my friend. "Her father's spirit is standing right next to me."

"I know," she replied. "I see him, too. You know what you have to do."

"We aren't here to do readings, and I don't want to step on anyone's toes, so I'm going to have to ask him to find another conduit to his daughter," I said, hoping the spirit would take the hint.

After the lecture, Nancy and I decided to eat at the Cassadaga Hotel. During our meal, Janice, the woman from the lecture, came in and ordered lunch. She sat at a table near us. I started getting the tingling sensation I experience when a spirit makes itself known to me. Her father's spirit was next to me again.

"Good Lord, this guy doesn't give up. What should I do, Nancy?" I asked.

"Go ahead. He's not going to leave you alone until you give her a message," Nancy said.

Nervously, I walked over to Janice's table. "I need to tell you something."

She looked up at me without saying a word.

"Your father asked me to tell you he's fine. He is in the Light."

Janice put down her sandwich. "Excuse me?"

"Please don't get angry with me, but when you walked in, your father's spirit came to me and said, 'Tell my daughter I'm in the Light. I'm happy, but her excessive grieving is holding me back from the next level.'"

"How do I know you're not full of crap?" she asked. "I mean, you could just be telling me what I wanna hear."

"He is giving me an image of you sitting alone before a mirror, in what looks like your bedroom. The mirror is on a small table, and there's a doily under it. This was just before his funeral. His spirit was with you, and he wants you to know this. You're holding a gold ring in your hand, and you're crying. There is major significance associated with this ring," I conveyed.

Her face turned red. I expected the worst, but she rose to her feet and gave me a hug. "Thank you so much. I just needed to know you were legit. That was my dad's wedding ring. What you described is exactly what happened. We buried him with that ring. It was my job to put the ring on his finger before the funeral. Looking at him in a coffin was the hardest thing I've ever had to do."

Relieved, I explained, "I was reluctant to speak to you, afraid maybe you might think I'm crazy—or get angry and yell at me."

"*Hello*—we're in Cassadaga!" Janice smiled and continued, "That's why I came here. I was hoping to hear from him. Thank you so much! He's right, though. I need to try and let go. I've been grieving so heavily. I kept feeling he was around me, and I just had to know for sure."

"He's definitely been with you. What you need to understand is that by letting go of the sorrow associated with his death, he can ascend to a higher level on the Other Side," I explained. "He needs you to know that he will always be with you. But, for your own healing, you have to move through this intense grief."

Because a loved one's death is such a traumatic experience, we can be overwhelmed by emotion. This opens us up psychically, since psychic activity is emotion-based. While in a hyperemotional state of grief, a person is more sensitive and more likely to sense the presence of a spiritual entity. This is known as clairsentience (clear feeling). People who experience clairsentience describe feeling the presence of a loved one around them. Like Janice, they cannot explain how, but they *know* that the spirit of their loved one is near.

PERHAPS THE MOST prevalent form of contact experience occurs during sleep. Unlike the surrealism typical of a dream, a visitation is a coherent experience. It feels different than a dream because it is a lucid conversation with a loved one. The quality of the image of the loved one is generally clearer than in a dream. Visitations have a rational beginning, middle, and end. Perhaps spirits prefer to make contact during sleep because the mind is freed from the awake-time chatter of daily life.

In the first sleeping visitation I had from my mother, I saw myself enter a modern-looking restaurant with white décor. The white walls had large glass picture windows. Billowy white clouds were visible through the windows. At the time, no one else was in the restaurant with me except for a woman sitting at a table in the corner. She looked young—about thirty-five years old. It was my mother. She looked great. Her eyes were clear. Her hair was black. She had no wrinkles on her face.

I sat down across from her at the table and asked, "You're on the Other Side, aren't you?"

"Yes."

"What are you doing over there?" I asked, realizing this experience was coherent.

She replied, "I'm very busy."

"Busy? Doing what?" I was excited to know.

"Learning," she replied. "It's all about growth of the soul and spiritual development." Then she said, "Mark, I'm sorry I died, because I know how upsetting it was for you. But don't worry, I'm fine and I'm happy. Please tell this to everyone in the family and ask them not to worry, because everything will be all right. They will see me when they come here."

Because she looked so healthy and young, I said, "You look beautiful."

She replied, "I'm working on looking younger."

Because this was in a lucid dream, I was aware enough to realize the contact was beginning to fade. Quickly I asked, "Mom, before you go, can you give me the Pick 6 winning lottery numbers?"

She raised her finger and pointed at me, scolding, "Mark, you know it doesn't work that way!" And then she was gone.

Soon my siblings and some of my psychically inclined friends experienced similar dreams in which my mother spoke to them. My phone rang frequently as they called to say, "You won't believe what happened last night!" However, I never mentioned to anyone that when I saw my mother in these visitations, she appeared to be only about thirty-five years old.

One morning, my brother, Earl Joseph, called me. "I had this dream, and Mom looked really young—like she was barely thirty-five years old!" Soon after that call, my sister, my father, and Nancy reported similar appearances in their dreams: Jeannie looked like she was in her thirties! Apparently, Mom's spirit was quite busy contacting everyone close to her and making a point of appearing youthful.

I have found that when a spirit initially comes through, the spirit usually appears as he or she did prior to passing. This seems to be for the purpose of validation. It is helpful to the medium and to the person having the reading in order to be able to identify the person easily. For example, if your grandmother was ninety years old when she died but came through looking twelve years old, chances are you would have no idea who she was.

I've had a number of spirits show up looking seventy years old at first, who then morph into looking thirty years old. Why? The answer is unclear, but it may be to prove that the spirit is in a beautiful place—free of illness, aging, and physical limitations. Most of the time, spirits want loved ones in the material world to know they are happy on the Other Side. Since they are now pure spiritual energy, spirits apparently have the ability to appear however they choose. Maybe it comes down to this: if we could all look great, why wouldn't we?

My friend Joan constantly has mediumistic experiences when she is asleep, mostly in the form of visitations. She and her husband, Mitch, were close friends with their neighbor Michael. When Michael's grandmother, Helen, died, Joan had a series of visitations in her sleep from Helen.

One day, Joan and Michael came to my office. Joan wanted to tell me, in detail, about the nature of the visitations she was having.

Michael said, "I don't know what to think about all this psychic stuff, but something weird's been going on. I need some advice. I've been friends with Joan for over twenty years. She said you'd know what to make of this, Mr. Anthony."

"What was it?" I wanted to know.

Joan said, "I dreamed that I was in a store, looking at shoes, and Helen came up to talk to me."

"I know there's more to this. What happened next?" I asked.

"It's what Helen said," Joan explained. "She said, 'Tell Mikey I said hello.'"

Michael chimed in. "No one calls me Mikey. My name is Michael—and that is what I want people to call me. I never even go by Mike, just Michael."

"And?" I asked.

"That's the weird thing. The only one who ever called me Mikey was my grandmother. She called me Mikey until I was eleven years old. After that, I said, 'Grandma, I don't want you to call me Mikey; call me Michael.' And she said, 'Okay, so now you're Michael—but to me you'll always be my little Mikey.' Joan never knew that. No one knows that."

This intrigued me. "What did she look like?" I asked Joan.

Joan seemed surprised. "Come to think of it, Helen looked about thirty years old, but I knew her voice right away. I recognized her face, except she seemed so young."

Michael interjected, "Joan didn't meet Grandma until she was in her late seventies!"

I BELIEVE THAT spirits can and do occasionally move physical objects to send us a message and to reach out to us. This is not an uncommon form of contact.

The object will always mean something to the person who notices it. After all, it is a form of communication. The object may be a personal item of sentimental value connected to the spirit when the person was alive, or it may be something with symbolic meaning to bring a connection to the spirit.

Bobby is one of my favorite clients. He was born and raised in rural Florida, and the best way to describe Bobby is the way he describes himself: "I'm a beer-drinking, gun-toting, pickup truck–driving, God-fearing redneck." One of the things I like about Bobby is that if he is your friend, he is your friend for life. Beneath the rough exterior, the waters run deep. He is extremely intelligent. He has also been the recipient of amazing contact experiences.

Bobby owns a landscaping business. One morning, while on a landscaping job, he was walking back to his truck. He unlocked the door, and on the dashboard he found the most perfect white hibiscus flower he'd ever seen. Startled, he wondered how it got there. Bobby asked his employee, "Did you put that white hibiscus on my dash?"

She said, "No, Bobby, the truck was locked, and you're the only one with a key. I have no idea how it got there."

Bobby was perplexed. Then his cell phone rang. It was his father, a man not prone to expressing emotion, and he was crying. Bobby stood in shock as he heard that his mother, Violet, had just died.

When Bobby told me about the flower, I was amazed. He looked intently at me and said, "I heard about you talkin' to dead people and all. How do you reckon that perfect white hibiscus got into my locked truck? I can't explain it."

"I think you can, Bobby," I responded. "It appeared at the precise moment you received the news of your mom's passing. What do *you* think that means?"

"I think it was a sign from her," he said as he looked away. I could hear the strain in his voice, and I knew he didn't want to break down in front of me.

"I agree. I also believe it was a sign. You're a man of the earth. You connect with nature and can bring forth life from what others might believe to be lifeless. What does a perfect white hibiscus mean to you?"

"It is a symbol of purity and life," he said slowly, "and here's how I know this: the flower only lasts one day before it wilts. This one lasted a month before it wilted. Ain't that remarkable?"

As far as Bobby was concerned, this was a message from the Other Side.

THE MANIPULATION OF electrical fields is a manifestation of spirit contact. The theory is that since spirits are energy, most likely energy with an electrical component, they are able to influence electrical devices.

Bobby seemed to have no lack of contact experiences, and he sought my advice again. One Saturday afternoon, he called me and asked me to come to his house. "There's something weird goin' on—you gotta see it," he said.

I followed Bobby into the bathroom, where Bobby said, "I really miss Mama." As soon as he said this, the lights began to do something unusual. One of the lights began to blink rapidly and the other began to fade and then slowly brighten. Bobby seemed amazed, exclaiming, "Ain't that weird?"

"Looks like you need to replace a few bulbs," I said. I didn't understand why he seemed so transfixed gazing at light bulbs.

"It ain't possible," Bobby said, with a twinge of fear in his voice.

"What, that you need to buy some light bulbs?" I joked.

"No," he replied with a frown. "Both of these here fixtures is on the same circuit."

"So?" I still did not grasp the significance of what had happened.

"This blinking and fading ain't possible. These bulbs is on the same circuit," he explained. "What that means is that if one is blinking, they should both be blinking. If one is fading, they should both be fading. They can't be doing different things at the same time. It ain't possible!"

"So this has never happened before?" I asked.

"Never," he said. "I've never seen anything like it, and it only happens when we're talkin' about Mama. Is Mama doin' this?"

"Let's find out," I said.

"You think we can?"

"Violet, is that you?" I asked, using his mother's name.

Immediately the blinking and fading stopped, and the lights returned to normal. Our eyes met. Bobby's mouth was hanging open—much the same way I'm sure mine was.

"This is freakin' me out!" Bobby exclaimed.

I received a call from Bobby two days later. This strange electrical anomaly had caused him to take the circuit apart several times. He had even called an electrician, who found that there was absolutely no problem with the circuit, the fixtures, or the bulbs.

"There ain't no explanation for why those bulbs is acting that way, unless—" He stopped in mid-sentence.

"Unless?" I asked.

"Unless something unexplainable was interfering with the electrical field," Bobby said.

"Such as the energy field of a spirit?" I asked.

"You're freakin' me out again, Mr. Anthony—I gotta go." Bobby hung up the phone.

Since spirits are energy, their influence over electrical fields extends beyond machinery. I believe this explains why some people (including myself) get a tingling sensation when a spiritual entity is present. Since a spirit is an energy field, the spirit can affect our electrical field, which results in our feeling cold chills. This physiological sensation may be interpreted as fear, even though spirits are not intending to frighten us. If a spirit can do that to a person, then why couldn't a spirit make two light bulbs on the same circuit do different things—one to blink and one to fade?

The manipulation of electrical fields can be one component of a contact experience. Spirits do not limit themselves to just one type of anomaly when contacting those here in the material world. Sometimes spirits will make themselves visible, especially to those who are capable of perceiving them.

My great-grandmother, Giovanna, was a particularly gifted psychic medium. She and her husband, Roberto, operated an Italian lemon ice factory in Newark, New Jersey, in the 1940s. They employed their entire extended family, who lived in a building next to the factory. Roberto was a workaholic who made sure the lemon ice business was in production day and night. He never took any time off and quite literally worked himself to death. In 1947, Giovanna found herself a widow.

Without Roberto to push the family to the extreme, the hours of operation at the Italian lemon ice factory had to be cut back. However, in the middle of the night, not long after Roberto passed, the entire family heard loud noises coming from the factory. They all rushed next door to see what had happened. Lights began flipping on all around the neighborhood. Soon, practically everyone in this Italian neighborhood was outside to see what was happening.

Giovanna and her children, grandchildren, siblings, cousins, neighbors, and friends flooded into the factory. All of the lemon ice machinery was running, but no one was in the building. They were amazed at what they saw. "How could this be?" "What turned on the machines?" Everyone had questions.

Giovanna knew the answer. She saw Roberto's spirit standing in the midst of the equipment. Her clairvoyant mediumistic ability enabled her to see him. She bellowed over the roar of the machines, "Roberto! You're dead! You don't have to work anymore!"

Abruptly, all of the machines stopped. As Roberto's spirit receded from Giovanna's view, an otherwordly silence filled the factory. The astonished crowd gaped at Giovanna.

She smiled politely at the crowd and, with a graceful wave of her arm, motioned for everyone to leave. The frightened onlookers all but ran for the door—and for once, no one in this boisterous Italian neighborhood had anything to say.

CLAIRVOYANT CONTACT EXPERIENCES occur when someone sees a spirit as if he or she is a living person. Such experiences are not unusual where a loved one in spirit may be seen, if only for a moment. Sometimes the visual image of the loved one is much more than a momentary flash, a snapshot, or a glimpse in one's peripheral vision. Although it might be easy to dismiss a clairvoyant contact experience as a grief-induced hallucination, it is not. It is real.

We can even have a clairvoyant contact experience without having an emotional connection to the spirit. They can be frightening for people who do not encounter spirits on a regular basis. However, even for those who do, it can still be unsettling.

My mother often spoke of her psychic experiences and was excited about learning as much as she could about using her gift. She was gregarious and often the focal point of attention in social settings. She spoke openly about her psychic and mediumistic experiences. On the other hand, my father, Earl, never discussed his psychic ability, regarding it as something dark and frightening. He avoided engaging in conversation about it, even with my mother. However, one day he didn't have a choice.

At a local diner, Earl and Jeannie had just ordered breakfast and were discussing how they were going to spend their day together. As she was taking a sip of coffee, Jeannie suddenly experienced a tingling sensation that she described as a "heightened awareness." She knew exactly what it was. And then she saw the spirit.

Beside their table, a presence approached—the spirit of a tall, black-haired woman wearing a long black-and-white checkered dress. The spirit had no visible face. Jeannie stared in horror, wondering why this faceless entity chose this particular time to approach her. This was not a familiar presence, and Jeannie thought it might be a wayward spirit looking for anyone who could perceive her—but, regardless, this entity frightened and unnerved her.

She tried to act as if the spirit was not there. Looking over at Earl, though, she saw he had a shocked expression on his face. His eyes were wide with fear; his mouth was agape. "Jeannie," he whispered. "There is a ghost standing next to us."

"You can see that?" Jeannie asked. "You can really see that, too?"

"Yes," Earl replied. He seemed almost annoyed. "You see her, too?"

"Earl, describe her to me," Jeannie coaxed, fascinated to know that Earl also saw this spirit.

"She's tall, wearing a black-and-white checkered dress, and this may sound crazy, but she has no face," Earl said slowly.

"You can see that she has no face, too?" Jeannie exclaimed, sitting up straight.

Earl asked, "Why did you bring that ghost here?"

Jeannie's dark eyes flashed from the spirit to Earl. "What exactly is that supposed to mean?"

"It's all that hocus-pocus stuff of yours."

Jeannie's temper began to flare. "*Hocus pocus?* How dare you ..."

"Jeannie, make her go away," Earl insisted. He was clearly nervous.

"How the hell am I supposed to do that? *I* didn't ask her to come here. She just came. *You* make her go away," Jeannie retorted.

Earl didn't know how to respond. By now, people at nearby tables were beginning to stare at them. He didn't want to argue about how to tell a spirit with no face, standing at their table in a crowded diner on a Sunday morning, to go away.

Jeannie wasn't sure what was irritating her more—a faceless spirit lingering at their table or her husband's insinuation that she was somehow responsible for the spirit being there.

As this awkward moment intensified, the server approached the table with their breakfast. She stepped right through the entity and put their meals on the placemats before them, shivering as if she felt a cold chill. Shrugging it off with a friendly smile, completely unaware, she asked, "Is there anything else I can get you all?"

Jeannie and Earl shook their heads. The spirit receded and faded out of view. They stared at each other. For the rest of their meal, neither one said another word.

SPIRITS WANT US to know the Other Side exists. They reach out and make contact with us in many different ways. Sometimes the contact is hard to explain; other times it is easy. However, spirits are always around us and always with us.

Contact experiences are real. Spirits are aware of what is going on with us in the material world. The fact that they are around us should not frighten us. The Other Side is another dimension that runs parallel to the dimension we physically exist in.

Everything in the universe vibrates at different speeds. Because we are physical, our vibration in the material world is slower than that of the spirit realm. When they believe it is necessary to do so, spirits can slow the speed of their vibration in order to make contact with us. Usually the contact is very subtle, so one must be sensitive in looking for it. Other times, the contact is more obvious.

The next time you are alone, thinking of a loved one who has passed, and you suddenly turn on the radio only to hear a song that brings back a vivid memory or sense the person's loving presence or glimpse a familiar smiling face or smell a recognizable scent or hear kind words in a beloved voice, you may ask yourself if your loved one is still with you.

The answer is—*yes*.

5

It's Nice to Know
We Are Never Truly Alone

*M*any people wrestle with feelings of loneliness and abandonment during bereavement. While we may feel lonely, it is essential to understand that we are never alone spiritually. Numerous spiritual entities are around us constantly to help us through our difficult times, such as when we grieve the loss of a loved one.

When I attended a media symposium in New York City, rumor got around that the "psychic lawyer" was present. People are curious about my work as a medium, and soon I was approached by several individuals with questions. One woman stands out in my mind. It was clear to me that she had recently sustained a loss. "Please," she asked, "can you tell me if there is a spirit around me?"

I responded, "The truth is, spirits are *always* around us."

This led to the questions: "What spirits are with me? Why are they here?"

"Spirits of loved ones are always looking out for us and remain connected to us through the power of love. We are all energetically connected," I explained.

The spirits of loved ones are often with us, but like us, they are not alone either. Our main spirit guide is always with us, as are other spirit helpers and teachers who might be angels and/or human spirits. Angels are a separate "species" distinctly different from spirits, who once inhabited a human body. They, like humans, are sentient beings created by God. However, angels have never existed in corporeal form and were created only as spiritual entities to act as messengers for God, working on God's behalf. In a sense, they are an extension of certain aspects of God's will and power.

Through the psychic sense of clairvoyance, I am able to see both angels and spirits, and each appears differently to me. Spirits of humans look like people and are usually somewhat transparent. Angels are humanoid in that they look similar to people; however, there are significant differences. As I perceive them, angels emanate light, appearing very bright. Sometimes they are so luminescent that all I can see is their radiance. Due to their extremely high level of spiritual development, their auras are brilliant. I don't believe angels have wings, but the way light emanates from their shoulder area makes it appear that they do. The intense color waves from their auric field could be interpreted as wings. I'm not sure if angels have a gender, although some look more male and others appear more female. There are different types of angels, all of whom work in harmony with human spirits. The most highly evolved angelic entities are referred to as the archangels: Michael, Raphael, Gabriel, and Uriel.

A person can also have a guide who is an angel, hence the term guardian angel. I have no certain knowledge whether or not each person is "assigned" an angel as a spirit guide; however, the assistance of angels is always accessible.

Other spiritual entities that are with us are the ascended masters. They are spiritual beings who have achieved their maximum grace or fulfillment according to the tasks assigned to them by God. This broad term is applied not only to certain angels but also to the spirits of people considered saints and others revered as holy.

Jesus is an extremely powerful ascended master. Other ascended masters include those who also perfected by living lives of holiness, such as Buddha, Krishna, Mary (the mother of Jesus), Mahatma Gandhi, Mother Teresa of Calcutta, Saint Francis of Assisi, Saint Anthony of Padua, Saint Jude Thaddeus, Saint Theresa of Avila, and Paramahansa Yogananda, to name just a few.

The ascended masters, who were once human, brought teachings of truth and light to us when they resided in the material world. They excelled during their life on earth, mastering their own life lessons. Now, from the Other Side, they are able to share their wisdom with us as well as with other spirits seeking to evolve to a higher level of development. Along with the archangels, these highly evolved ascended masters inspire us toward spiritual growth in their wish to spread peace, enlightenment, and truth.

Ascended masters and archangels are multidimensional beings—their presence transcends time and space. This may explain why they are able to manifest in several places at the same time to deliver messages and heal people in the material world. From the earthly perspective, we are fortunate to have their help and support to bring us the awareness of the love that is God.

My friend Nancy, whom I mentioned earlier in the book, is a firsthand recipient of the power of God's healing energy and love as manifested through an ascended master. When she was in her twenties, Nancy was in a horrific car accident. Her body was badly mangled; her legs were crushed. She endured immense physical pain, twelve surgeries, and had to be in leg casts for seven years. Her doctors told her she would never walk again.

Despite what her doctors said, Nancy never lost her faith. Although she grieved the loss of the use of her legs, she prayed constantly for God's help and healing. Then one July day, when she was still confined to casts, she felt an incredible spiritual presence fill her room. "This presence felt like total love surrounding me," Nancy recalled, "and then I saw someone standing at the foot of my bed. It was Jesus."

"You will walk in October," Jesus told her—and then he vanished.

Several of her family members and friends doubted the validity of her story, but Nancy remained convinced she had received a visitation from Heaven.

After seven excruciating years, her leg casts were finally removed in September. Now she could use a wheelchair. Then, in the first week of October, Nancy tried to stand up. She walked a few steps. Every day thereafter, she could walk a little farther. Soon she regained the use of her legs. Her doctors were astonished and could not provide a rational medical explanation for what Nancy describes as a miracle.

"I know I'm never alone," Nancy often explains. "Jesus is my guide."

It is interesting to note that since that time, Nancy's psychic abilities have intensified. She is an excellent psychic medium and uses her ability to conduct energy healings.

ANGELS AND GUIDES are here to assist you, not to control you. You can choose to listen to them—or not. You may have all kinds of spiritual assistance and guidance from your spirit guide, spirit helpers, teachers, family members, and ascended masters, but the decision to follow their guidance is up to you. This is one way that free will comes into play.

Each of us has a life plan that is preordained. There is an appointed day we will be born and an appointed day we will die. What we do in between depends on us. We have several lessons and a life mission to complete. We are spiritual entities having a temporary existence in a physical body. The reason we are here is to learn the lessons that come with having a physical life. When living in the material world, our priority is to have a human experience. When we are finished here, our body dies, and we return to spirit.

One day Jackson, a potential client, walked into my office. He hadn't called ahead of time and didn't have an appointment but was insistent on seeing me right away. Fortunately, my schedule was clear. Jackson was a tall, muscular African-American man who didn't seem like the type of person who would be easily intimidated or frightened. However, he was visibly upset and seemed depressed.

"So what brings you here today, Jackson?" I asked.

"I killed a boy," he said. I could see he was using all of his self-control to keep from shedding tears. "It was an accident; I didn't mean to do it."

Although this is the type of story every criminal defense attorney routinely hears, this man seemed different. I felt his genuine remorse and sorrow. Jackson also radiated a depth of goodness, and I found it hard to believe he would intentionally harm anyone.

"What were you charged with?" I asked.

"Careless driving and improper left turn," Jackson replied.

His answer surprised me, since these are civil traffic infractions, not criminal charges. "Was this a traffic accident?" I asked.

"Yes," he said, wiping tears from his eyes with a tissue. "I was attending a funeral for my boss's mother. As I was leaving the church, I pulled out onto the main street. Suddenly, a speeding motorcycle appeared out of nowhere. I tried to avoid it, but the boy on the motorcycle was going so fast. He slammed into the front driver's side of my car. I actually made eye contact with him at that moment. I saw the fear in that poor boy's eyes. It was horrible. He must have been thrown a hundred feet after hitting my car." With that, Jackson's control broke down, and he began to sob.

"Good lord, I'm so sorry," I said, overwhelmed by this tragic chain of events. Trying to maintain a professional demeanor, I continued, "Do you have a police report?"

He showed me the police report, and it looked to me like Jackson happened to be in the wrong place at the wrong time when he pulled out in front of the motorcycle. The police estimated the motorcycle was going at least thirty miles above the speed limit. In my opinion as an attorney, Jackson was not at fault in the collision.

We talked for over an hour about the case, and I finally got him to calm down. He was completely guilt-ridden over this tragedy. He said he hadn't slept a full night since it happened. He wondered how the boy's family could ever forgive him. He also told me how totally alone he felt. "Even my family has abandoned me," Jackson said. "I need to prove it wasn't my fault. Maybe then I can start to forgive myself."

"I'm curious; what made you decide to come to my office?"

"That is the really weird part," he explained. "I kept asking myself, who can help me with this case? Who will understand? Who will believe me? And then I was driving by your office, and—please don't laugh at me when I tell you this—I was directed here."

"Are you sure you don't mean *referred* here?" I asked.

"No, I mean *directed*," he said sternly. He continued, "A voice told me to come here."

"A voice?" I inquired. "Tell me about it."

"Do you believe in guardian angels?"

"Actually, I do," I assured him.

"That's why I'm here. My guardian angel directed me to see you," he said.

"I understand."

"You do?" He sounded surprised. "You don't think that's weird?"

"I don't think that's weird, Jackson. I believe in guardian angels."

"Thank you," he replied, looking somewhat relieved, and then added, "I guess it's nice we're never alone."

After he left, I gave my notes to my assistant, Melissa, so she could open the file. I could see the startled expression on her face as she finished reading. Then she joked, "Did you start advertising on the Other Side and not tell me?"

SO MANY PEOPLE grapple with feelings of loneliness. Such feelings are intensified after the death of a loved one. It is hard to accept the idea of not seeing someone who was such a huge part of your life. It is not unusual to feel abandoned. Spirits are aware of these feelings, and they want you to know they *never* abandon you.

Penny contacted me about having a reading over the telephone. Before I conduct a reading, I believe it is necessary to explain to the client how I receive information. Initially, I sense the presence of a spiritual entity and whether it is a male or female. Then, I get a sense of the spirit's relationship to the client; for example, it might be a grandfather, mother, sibling, or friend. During the reading, I will begin to receive messages, which I usually hear in the form of thoughts. I also receive physical sensations that indicate the nature of the person's physical passing. This information is transmitted to me by the spirit and is never meant to be upsetting, although sometimes it can be. No one ever forgets how a loved one died. A spirit knows this, which is why the cause of death is an important fact since it can validate the spirit's identity. Due to the traumatic impact a death can have, it is understandable that a survivor may spend a lifetime grieving over how a loved one died. However, one of the reasons a spirit reaches out to communicate is to alleviate suffering by letting a loved one know that life exists beyond physical death. The spirit of a loved one will never communicate anything harmful to someone here; rather, the spirit presents evidence to help validate his or her identity.

In the reading for Penny, I felt a male presence come through. He was around thirty years old, and I felt he might be a son. I described his physical appearance when alive, and she acknowledged that he was, in fact, her son. I liked her son's spirit right away. He was a nice, kind man. He loved his mother very much—and I communicated this to her.

Then, I felt a sudden impact to my chest and face. I could also taste blood in my mouth. Although I knew what this meant, I was reluctant to give these details to Penny. When possible, I try to be diplomatic with clients, so I explained, "It feels as if he may have died in a car collision."

"Yes, he did," she confirmed.

"He wants you to know that it hurt only for a few seconds before he was released. He wants me to tell you not to worry about that anymore," I conveyed. This is an example of a spirit coming to the rescue, knowing that his mother had been afraid he had suffered.

"I've agonized for years wondering about that. Thank you," she said. I could hear the relief in her voice.

I received another message: "The maple tree."

"Oh god!" she exclaimed.

"You don't need to come to the maple tree anymore," Penny's son wanted her to know.

"When he lost control of his car and hit a maple tree, the car flipped and went into a lake next to the road. I go there all the time. I stand there and wonder why," Penny explained.

"He knows you feel alone," I told her. "He also knows you feel abandoned by him. His wife and children are coping with that same abandonment."

"I miss him so much. His wife and kids do feel abandoned. Life feels so empty without him," Penny confessed.

"You feel his hand on your left shoulder sometimes when you stand alone at the maple tree, don't you?" I asked.

"Dear Lord!" Penny exclaimed. "Is that really him?"

"Yes, he reaches out to you. He is adamant that he doesn't want you to go to the maple tree anymore."

"Are there any messages for his wife or his children?" Penny asked.

"This is interesting," I said. "He knows his daughter can see him."

"It's true, then!" Penny said excitedly. "His daughter always talks about seeing Daddy!"

"Sounds like you have a medium in the family," I added.

JULIE INTERVIEWED FOR a job at my office. She indicated that she had recently relocated to Florida. During the interview, I saw the spirit of a large, heavyset man standing next to her. He was wearing a tweed jacket with a white shirt and a tie. I sensed a pain in my chest. It seemed as if the spirit wanted me to know he had died of a heart attack.

I asked Julie why she had moved to Florida. She grew silent and then said, "My husband died. He was a lawyer, and after his death, I had to get away from Illinois, where we lived. I wanted to start over."

It became clear to me that the spirit was her husband and that he wanted me to hire Julie. I tried not to smile as I realized I'd never received a reference from the Other Side before. This was definitely one of the more interesting job interviews I'd conducted.

Then Julie interjected, "I'd like to ask you a question, Mr. Anthony."

"Sure, go ahead," I responded.

"Is it true you are a medium? I mean, that's not why I'm here—I really want the secretarial job—but I heard things."

"Does that bother you?" I asked.

"No, it doesn't. In fact, I was hoping you might consider doing a reading for me," she confided.

I agreed, but only on the condition she not tell me anything else about her personal background or her husband. I do this to ensure that the information that comes through in a reading is not influenced by anything I might know ahead of time.

About a week after she started with my office, I conducted the reading. Julie's maternal grandfather came through first. He appeared thin and physically worn out from a lifetime outdoors. "This man was a smoker and drinker and used a lot of, shall we say, expletives," I told Julie.

She smiled. "That's definitely Grandpa. He liked his gin and cussed a lot. He loved me so much. I was crushed the day he died."

"I sense he was a good and loving man. He adored you, and he knows you miss him." Julie nodded in agreement.

"Now his wife, your grandmother, is coming through. She was shorter than your grandfather. She had a very round face and wore little wire-framed glasses. She liked to bake you sugar cookies and have you sit on her lap when you were a little girl," I explained.

"Hi, Grandma," Julie said softly.

Then Julie's husband made his presence known. I recognized him from his appearance at her interview. "He wants you to know that it was not your fault he died. He never listened to you about his eating habits."

"That's for sure. I tried to cook healthfully, but he always snuck fast food behind my back. His doctor told him he'd have a heart attack if he didn't change his eating habits. I tried to help him—he wouldn't listen," she said.

"He also wants you to know he had no control over when he was going to die. He says his heart gave out and that it was quick and painless," I conveyed.

"That's good to know," Julie said, looking down.

"He's sorry about how that turned out, very sorry—he keeps repeating that he didn't mean to do that to you," I explained.

"It was the worst time of my life," Julie said. "Grandpa died on a Monday. I was devastated by his death and couldn't bear the thought of going to his funeral, which was three days later. Then Thursday morning, the day of his funeral, I woke up next to my husband, Jim. Except," she paused, staring blankly, "Jim had died in his sleep. He was dead in bed next to me."

This was one of those situations where it was difficult for me to find the right words to say, so I silently asked Jim's spirit to help me out.

"Jim is switching tracks now," I explained. "He is showing me several images of his life with you. There is a blue house on a lake and a sailboat."

This made Julie smile a little. "That was our escape—the house on the lake. We loved to sail. We were very happy then."

I was thankful and relieved that Jim's spirit had come to my rescue. I continued conveying the images he presented to me. "He is showing me an image of the two of you at night, next to the lake, roasting marshmallows around a fire."

"We spent many evenings doing that," Julie said softly.

"Jim is holding up a marshmallow that is on fire. It's a small flame. He is saying, 'Do not put your fire out before its time,'" I conveyed.

Julie stared at me. Her dark eyes were beyond tears.

"Your grandmother says, 'To do that would ruin your life plan.'" I added, "Julie, it sounds to me like your family on the Other Side is pretty concerned about you."

It became clear these were messages of warning for Julie, who admitted she had been contemplating suicide.

"They abandoned me! I mean, Grandpa *and* Jim, in the same week? And Jim had to go and die in bed next to me! Why didn't he listen to me? Why didn't he listen to his doctor?" Julie asked. I could feel her hurt and anger.

"They definitely don't want you to harm yourself, which is why they're reaching out to you now," I explained.

"Without Jim, Grandpa, and Grandma, I felt so isolated in Illinois. I even thought about how I was going to kill myself," Julie confessed.

"I can't even begin to imagine what you've been through. And I also realize that contacting their spirits isn't the same as having them physically here. Yet that doesn't mean they are not a part of your life. They love you so much, and they've reached out to help you. They don't want you to cut your life short," I told her.

"I understand," she said, regaining her composure. "I always felt they were with me. Part of the reason I moved to Florida was to start over. Since I've been here, I have realized that committing suicide isn't the answer."

Julie seemed to make a lot of progress in Florida, and after about six months she moved to another job. On her last day at my office, she told me she had accepted that she must endure the pain of loss and resolve her grief issues. She also said it brought her such comfort knowing she was never really alone and that her family on the Other Side was watching over her. I admire her insight and fortitude.

PSYCHICS HAVE THE same responsibilities as everybody else. We have to earn a living. We have to raise our children. We cope with all the stress and rigors of everyday life. What makes us different is our belief that there is more to our existence than what can be perceived by the five physical senses. For the most part, we listen to our spirit guides. A large part of psychic ability is learning to listen to those quiet, subtle messages and signs. Occasionally, the intervention of a spirit guide is much more direct.

One day in early 1953, my mother, Jeannie Anthony, was coming back from the grocery store with my sister, Roxanne, who was two and a half years old. Jeannie had a grocery bag in one arm and Roxanne in the other. It was a cold, snowy winter day in Newark. The wind was howling, creating a subzero windchill. Visibility was limited. Shivering and exhausted, Jeannie just wanted to get to her warm home with little Roxanne. Although she couldn't see more than a few feet in the snowstorm, she thought the street was clear, so she crossed it and headed toward her house.

Suddenly, a bus emerged through the blinding snowstorm just a few feet away, heading straight toward them. As the bus rapidly bore down, Jeannie froze in place, fearing this was the end.

Before she could scream, Jeannie felt incredibly strong hands grab the two of them. She gasped as they were lifted up and tossed with immense speed out of the way of the bus. She and Roxanne fell safely into the soft snow on the sidewalk. The hissing bus roared on past them.

Despite the shock of having almost been run over by a bus in the fierce storm, Jeannie had the oddest sensation: she felt a great sense of love surrounding her. On the snow-covered sidewalk, with her crying child beside her and her groceries tossed about, Jeannie grabbed her baby, sat up, and looked for someone to thank for saving their lives. No one was there.

Slowly, she rose to her feet and looked down at her groceries. Cans, some fresh vegetables, and a few broken jars were strewn on the sidewalk. In that moment, she understood. Tears of gratitude flooded her eyes as she clutched the weeping child in her arms. With the freezing wind howling all about her, Jeannie looked up toward Heaven to thank God for their lives. She knew she and Roxanne had been saved from certain death not by a human hand but by divine intervention.

We all have a time to live and a time to die. While we do have free will, we also are following a life plan. Generally, an angel or a guide will not intervene directly in our lives. Normally, they influence us by presenting us with feelings, ideas, thoughts—even notions, hunches, or nudges—in order to guide us, but the decisions and actions are up to us. That is the nature of free will. Everything happens in divine order, but when something interferes with divine order, then the Divine intervenes on our behalf. In my mother's case, a cold and dreary day in 1953 was not to be the day she and her child would cross over. A spiritual entity under the direction of God's divine will saw to that.

IN MY WORK as a medium, I've come across several people who have told me about similar experiences—they believe they were pulled out of harm's way by an unseen force. Some of these people were skeptics and atheists who never gave the spirit realm much credence. However, their opinions changed after a spirit came to their rescue. What these events prove to me is that spirit guides are always at work around us. When our life plan is about to be altered, a spirit may intervene.

Please do *not* test this theory by putting yourself in harm's way to see if an angel or spirit guide will save you. Live your life; try to cope with and accept all of the difficulties and trials that are thrown in your path. My mother often joked, "When life gives you lemons, and it often does, make Italian lemon ice."

Life can be brutal, and we often wonder why bad things happen to good people. Remember the people in this chapter—how their lives were shattered through no fault of their own and how, when they least expected it, a helping hand from the Other Side made all the difference. It's nice to know we are never truly alone.

6

From a Physical to a
Spiritual Relationship

*T*he Roman philosopher Seneca once said, "The day which we fear as our last is but the birthday of eternity." It is a privilege to have a physical life here in the material world. We come into this life for a reason and must endure all of the life lessons presented to us. When our mission here is completed, we cross to the Other Side and begin a new phase of our soul's journey. Physical death *is* our birth into eternity.

The disadvantage of living in the material world is that our perspective is limited to the physical realm. What exists beyond our ability to perceive with our five physical senses is considered the unknown. It is fear of the unknown that often leads us to believe that the person who physically died is lost forever. Yet the spirits who cross to the Other Side are anything but lost. A whole new world has opened to them. They are evolving and progressing in ways we cannot yet comprehend.

When a loved one dies, the relationship with that person is transformed from a physical relationship to a purely spiritual relationship. That is not to say that two people cannot be connected spiritually in life. I am referring to what occurs after a loved one crosses over. The relationship evolves. Once on the Other Side, spirits have a way of assisting and connecting with us when they deem it necessary to do so. Even after a spirit's passing and ascendance into the Light, a spirit still retains the capability to be with us. This means that spirits are aware of what is happening in our lives, as a young man named Riley came to realize.

Riley was referred to me for a mediumistic reading by a friend. Although I routinely counsel people from all walks of life, Riley wasn't what I expected of someone seeking contact with the Other Side. Instead, he looked like one of the criminal clients that I represent in my law practice. I knew he'd served hard time in prison even before he told me so. He was a physically large and muscular man who stood nearly six and a half feet tall. His face and arms were covered with tattoos, some of which I recognized as being indicative of gang membership. Among his many tattoos, he had *666* tattooed on one side of his neck and the image of an AK-47 assault rifle on the other side of his head. However, I found his gold-capped front teeth, which gave him a sinister smile, most intimidating.

He came to my office with his sister. She seemed very open to spirit contact and wanted to observe the reading but not participate. I told her I had no problem with her observing.

Gruffly, Riley started with, "I don't know if I believe this stuff."

"What you believe is up to you," I explained. "If you don't want to do this, you don't have to."

"Nah, I'll give it a shot. Go ahead—show me what you got," he said, flashing his eerie golden smile.

Two spirits came through initially. One felt like a father figure in Riley's life. He wanted to apologize to Riley, who abruptly stated, "No idea who that is."

Next, a younger man about Riley's age came through. It appeared that he had been full of rage while he was in the material world. I told Riley it looked to me like this man had died in a motorcycle accident. He said Riley needed to change the direction of his life.

"Nah, don't know him either," Riley said.

"I guess we're getting nowhere with this," I told him.

"I want to hear from my grandmother," Riley said, baring his gold teeth. "That's why I'm here. I don't care about those other people—get me my grandmother."

I had to tell to him that I don't conjure up or summon anyone. If a spirit wants to come through, it is the spirit's choice.

"What a load of—"

"Hold on," I said as another spirit made contact. "There's an older woman here—about seventy-three years old. She died of what feels like breast cancer. She also had heart problems."

Upon hearing this, Riley's entire demeanor changed. He didn't look quite so fierce now. He sank back into the chair across from me. "Yeah, that sounds like her."

This spirit gave me some information that was not quite so easy to convey. "She is talking about you now," I said, stalling for time.

"What's she saying?" he asked, leaning forward.

"This is about you. She is giving me physical sensations about something going on in your life. I'm feeling pinpricks in my left arm," I explained. "Now it feels as if there is a warm fluid moving through my arm and into my liver. She is indicating there is a connection between your left arm, what is being injected into it, and your liver."

"What's that supposed to mean?" he said, leaning closer.

"Let's ask your grandmother what her message is for you," I suggested.

"Yeah, I'd like to know," Riley said.

"She said she knows you feel alone since she died," I conveyed.

"Gran was the only mother I ever had," Riley stated.

"She also says that she wants you to stop—forgive me— she wants you to stop shooting up," I told him.

"Gran knows I'm shooting? I mean, uh, used to shoot," he said as his eyes scanned the room.

"I'm just relaying what she is communicating to me," I tried to explain.

"Shooting heroin can give you hepatitis. I suppose you think I look like someone who shoots up, huh?" he said menacingly. I could feel his rage and anger building.

"Stop it, Riley!" his sister interjected. "You've got hepatitis, and obviously Gran knows it."

"She also says you have a good mind and are intelligent and, if you stay clean, you can have a good life," I relayed.

"She thinks I can?" he asked. I could now see that all the macho bravado he had been projecting was just to cover up what was once a frightened little boy abandoned by his parents.

"She also says she knew you better than anyone. She always knew how to get around your, shall we say, temper."

"Yeah, she did," he said. "Thanks. Later, dude," he stood up and walked out of my office. His sister apologized for his rude behavior and left a few moments later.

Oftentimes, I don't understand the full extent of the messages from the Other Side or the relevance of who it is that comes through to communicate. The messages are not meant for me; they are meant for the recipient. It certainly helps if I have a cooperative recipient. Riley was not cooperative, and, given his background, I understood that.

The next day, Riley's sister called me. She wanted to thank me and to tell me about the two men who had come through initially. The first man was their stepfather, who was an abusive alcoholic. She explained how he used to physically beat them. He died from a drug overdose. "It's good to hear that he's at least sorry for being such a rotten father," she remarked.

Their mother had abandoned them not long after that and ended up in prison for possession of heroin. She was released from prison when Riley was eleven years old, and neither he nor his sister had seen their mother since.

"I'm curious: who was the young man who died in a motorcycle accident?" I asked.

"That was our cousin," she told me. "He was a gang member when he was killed. Riley confessed on the way home that hearing from our cousin really freaked him out, but he'd never admit that to you. That's why he said he didn't know who it was. He also freaked out over Gran knowing about the hepatitis and his shooting up. He said what you told him made him think that maybe she's really still around."

For many people like Riley, grief interferes with the idea of a spiritual relationship with a deceased loved one. We can no longer talk on the telephone, sit down to talk, have a meal together, or share a laugh. At the very least, this reading made Riley consider the possibility his grandmother's spirit could still be with him.

WE DO NOT think of the universe as stagnant because the universe is constantly changing. Look at the world around you and ask yourself—is it the same as it was a year ago, or five or fifty years ago?

Nothing stays the same. For those of us in the material world, physical death is but a painful reminder of this constant change. Experiencing the death of a loved one radically alters our world. Yet that is the nature of the universe—ever changing, forever evolving.

Once on the Other Side, spiritual beings continue to grow. They can assist other spirits as well as work with those of us who are still in the material world. Spirits have missions, which include reaching out to help and guide us from the Other Side.

TONYA, WHOM I'VE mentioned earlier in the book, is an eighty-five-year-old woman whom I've known for years. Many times I have represented her fifty-two-year-old son, who was always in trouble for selling drugs. Tonya usually bailed him out. However, I always liked Tonya and was surprised when she told me that she had an interest in mediumship.

"Even though I'm Jewish and not supposed to do this, Mark, I want to give it a try," Tonya told me at the start of the reading.

She had a good sense of humor, and it was a pleasure connecting with several of her relatives. These spirits had an almost frenetic energy. Most of Tonya's family did, except for the next spirit who came through.

This spirit was a male energy. He was calm, focused, and extremely intelligent. He felt like a son. I described him to her. Tonya looked very sad as she said, "That was my first-born. He was my pride and joy—not like the other one," she confided.

I felt a pain and the sensation of blood rushing to my head. Her son's spirit was communicating to me how he had passed. I could see he had taken some type of pills, since I saw a prescription bottle. However, his death was not connected to drugs. "There was some problem in his head," I explained to Tonya.

"He took medication for high blood pressure. He died of a brain aneurysm," Tonya told me. "That was the day my world ended."

"I sense that he was a wonderful and loving son. He is showing me how he gave you little presents all the time."

"He was so thoughtful that way," Tonya said with a smile.

"This is interesting—he says you don't like red roses, so instead he gave you little bouquets of mums and lilies," I conveyed.

"That's true, he always sent me flowers. Can't stand roses," Tonya admitted. "You think my other son would even think to send me flowers?"

"He is saying how your son here always looked up to him," I explained.

"He did. I just wish he would act more like his older brother," Tonya said, obviously very upset.

"Spiritually, he was by your side as you mourned his passing. He is showing how, night after night, you would cry in your room. He was there with you. He also acknowledges that on his birthday every year, he knows that you honor and remember him."

"I do," she said.

"He knows that every candle you light at Chanukah, you do in his memory," I relayed.

"I'm so happy he knows about his birthday and Chanukah," Tonya said, sobbing softly.

"He especially liked this one meal you would make. It's a chicken dish you baked for him. You made the chicken with paprika. And there were peeled potatoes—he's making it a point to emphasize the potatoes."

"That was his favorite dish, and those potatoes are my secret recipe; everyone calls them Tonya's Taters," she acknowledged tearfully.

"This reading is making me hungry," I said, trying to lighten the tension a bit before I continued. "He especially loved the dessert. There's a crisp apple strudel—I can even taste the cinnamon in it and the crunchy crust."

"The wrong son died!" Tonya cried suddenly. "Why did it have to be him? Why couldn't it have been that drug addict, good-for-nothing boy of mine? Why did God take the good one?"

"Your son on the Other Side has a response," I conveyed.

"What?" she asked, realizing that she'd expressed her innermost, secret feelings.

"We exist forever. Life goes on forever," I said, relaying her son's message.

"Really?" she exclaimed. "This is astonishing. I've been wondering since he died if there really is an afterlife. I just can't bring myself to believe."

"He says that is what he wanted you to know, and he has one final message for today."

"What? Tell me, please," she begged.

"He will always be with you."

This reading was an example of a spirit reaching out to console his mother, who had been left behind. He knew of her doubts about life after death and answered them before she could even ask the question. Tonya saw that, while her son may no longer have been physically part of her life, he was still involved spiritually.

WHILE I DO not presume to be an expert about the Other Side, and I don't know if anyone in the material world is, I have been given some insights. The Other Side is not some far-off, distant place. Rather, it is another dimension coexisting simultaneously with the dimension in which we exist. Because we live in the material world and are solid objects, our vibrational frequency is at a much slower and lower rate than the vibration of spiritual entities. Since spirits are essentially pure energy, they vibrate at a much higher frequency.

Perhaps the reason they can come to us so quickly is because their dimension runs concurrent with ours. In order for a spirit to make his or her presence known to us, the spirit must lower his or her vibrational frequency to a level where we have a frequency match. It is during these frequency matches that we are capable of contact experiences with those on the Other Side.

It appears that there are several levels to the Other Side. Spirits are concerned with and have the objective of ascending higher into the Light. My contact with spirits indicates that once you cross over to the Other Side and go into the Light, that is not the end. They do not sit on clouds playing harps; rather, they are quite busy. It appears there are different dimensions on the Other Side. Ascending higher into the Light may not necessarily mean higher in the sense of distance but in vibration and frequency. From what spirits tell me, it is an amazing place. This was one of the messages communicated by a spirit to Elaine.

Elaine asked for a reading because her son, Josh, had died six months earlier of a drug overdose. Prior to his death, he had just been released from a drug rehabilitation program and initially seemed to be doing well until he started using drugs again. As a lawyer, I'm sad to say this is a sequence of events I have witnessed many times. His mother was understandably devastated and needed some insight into the circumstances surrounding her son's passing.

Communicating with Josh was interesting because I was given the privilege of glimpsing his use of color, sensations, and impressions in expressing himself. Spirits maintain quite a bit of their human uniqueness and individuality. In his communication from the Other Side, Josh expressed himself as an artistic and conceptual person.

"He had a gift for everything of a creative nature—from painting to pottery to acting. He was funny and, at times, overly dramatic," I explained.

"He liked being the center of attention," Elaine agreed.

Josh showed me an image of himself as a child. It was clear that mother and son had a close relationship. Josh indicated that Elaine had performed many of the tasks that are traditionally reserved for a father, such as teaching him to ride a bicycle. She indicated these pieces of information were accurate.

"He liked giving you jewelry. There are two pieces he wants you to acknowledge. One is a gold bracelet with a red stone in it. The other is a necklace with white stones that look like pearls," I conveyed.

"I still have the bracelet. I lost the necklace. It had white stones, but they weren't pearls," Elaine noted.

"Josh is showing me how he passed," I said. "Are you sure you want to hear this?"

"Yes," Elaine said. I could see the tension in her face.

"I feel a draining sensation throughout my body. His head is clouded, as if he is losing control. And then he went into cardiac arrest," I explained.

Elaine nodded as tears rolled down her cheeks.

"Josh wants to make it very clear that this was not intentional," I relayed.

"Was it my fault? Could I have prevented his death?" Elaine wanted to know.

"There was nothing you could do," was the reply. "He says that it was his time to go. It was not your fault. Josh is showing me a large grandfather clock that makes a deep sound when it chimes. This image is his way of saying it was his time."

"Could anything have been done to save him?" Elaine asked.

"No. Josh indicates his life was full of anxiety. He was a sad person. He wants to make it clear that his new life on the Other Side is so much better. He is now giving me images of a pure waterfall washing away the pain. The water is flowing into a deep pool of dark blues and greens, symbolizing the depth of his nature and that now he is at peace," I explained.

"What else does he want me to know?" Elaine asked softly.

"He wants you to know he shrugged off his body and his anxiety like one shrugs off an old shirt. He is glad to be free of his pain." I continued with, "Now he is showing me green grass, blue sky, and yellow sun. He indicates the green symbolizes healing; the blue, serenity; and the yellow, happiness. This is his message to you. He wants you to heal, to find serenity, and to know happiness again."

"I wish I could," she said. "Where is he?"

"This is bizarre." I saw a strange image.

"What?" Elaine asked.

"I see a flying carpet," I said. "Does that mean anything to you?"

"A flying carpet?" Elaine looked puzzled. "Can you get more?"

"Now I hear a song—'It's a whole new world' from the movie *Aladdin*. He is explaining that his life on the Other Side is a whole new world and a wonderful adventure," I explained.

"That was his favorite movie and favorite song when he was a little boy," Elaine confided, smiling.

I felt privileged to connect with such a spirit. The conceptual nature of Josh's communication was challenging, yet it was a pleasure to experience the beautiful images he conveyed, especially the flying carpet. Although the sensation only lasted a few seconds, I got the impression I was personally standing on a flying carpet, feeling the wind rush past me as I saw the world zip by colorfully below. He wanted me to be able to convey to his mother that he was free of his mental and physical pain.

I can only imagine that, for spirits, it must be challenging to communicate, even when working with an experienced medium. For those who are not mediums, the contact from a spirit may be misunderstood. A spirit will reach out to us or we may feel the presence of the spirit, but most people do not know how to respond. Feeling a spirit's presence may be interpreted as grief-induced imagination or it may trigger additional pain and sadness. The spirit is trying to tell a loved one not to worry—the spirit is near and, eventually, you both will be reunited on the Other Side. Often this communication is completely misunderstood.

This may be analogous to communicating with a deaf person. You communicate by speaking English, and the other person communicates through American Sign Language. Neither one of you understands the other's language. The deaf person may get a sense of what you want but cannot be sure. However, if you learn to sign, you may both be able to communicate more directly.

Spirits are connected to us through love. They hear us. They feel our emotions. When we mourn for them, they feel our pain. When we pray for them, they hear our prayers. When we honor and remember them, they feel that, as well. And, when we need them, they may come to our rescue in their own way, from the Other Side.

WHEN CROSSING OVER, some spirits may be more elevated than others. What they have done in the material world has a direct bearing on what happens when they cross to the Other Side. Outstanding individuals such as Buddha, Saint Francis, Gandhi, and Mother Teresa will most likely enter at a higher frequency than most people. Because they were so evolved and had such a close connection to their spirituality and to God, and accomplished so many life lessons, they ascended to a higher vibration. However, spirits also indicate to me that once they are on the Other Side, they can and do continue to evolve. This is the natural progression of the soul.

A question arises about the souls of people who never had the opportunity to live a full life here in the material world. Do those spirits progress and evolve? The answer is yes, they do progress, since spirits are immortal.

I've conducted several readings for women who have miscarried. The spirit of the baby is quite capable of communicating, since a spirit exists independently of the body to which he or she was to be attached. The ability of a spirit to communicate is not predicated on having been born and growing to maturity. All souls are immortal and have existed since Creation.

Bonita had seen me speak about mediumship and life after death at a civic group. She called me for a reading since she believed it would be an interesting experience. I found Bonita to be a delight during our time together. Several of her relatives from the Other Side communicated; however, there was one she hadn't expected to hear from.

"A spirit of a young girl is coming through," I explained.

Bonita suddenly looked perplexed and asked, "How young?"

"Really young, tiny—a baby," I described. "She says she's your daughter."

"I miscarried years ago," Bonita said. "It was a little girl. How is it possible she can communicate?"

"Her message is that there is no limbo," I conveyed. "She's in the company of angels."

"That's odd. I haven't thought about limbo since I was a child. But this makes sense," she said.

"How so?" I asked.

"As a Catholic, I was taught that babies who died before they were baptized remained in a place called limbo. It isn't a negative place, but it isn't Heaven and it certainly isn't Hell," Bonita told me. "Does she know I've always prayed for her?"

"Yes, and she wants you to know she shines like a star," I relayed the spirit's message.

I'm not sure why, but when the spirits of babies make themselves known to me, they actually do shine like a star. Maybe it is an identifying piece of information communicated to symbolize that this spirit is that of a baby. Yet I do know spirits are ageless, and maybe it is done for more practical reasons. If the spirit of a baby showed up looking like she would have at age thirty, no one could recognize her. Perhaps it has something to do with that entity's spiritual purity, since that spirit has not been affected by a recent material-world existence.

Bonita and I talked for some time after the reading. She was amazed that her miscarried daughter knew her. I explained that while Bonita may not have gotten to know her daughter in the material world, they still have a spiritual relationship. Bonita was thrilled to know that her daughter heard her prayers.

Spirits definitely are aware that we pray for them. Note that I say pray *for* them and not *to* them. Prayer is an intensive form of spiritual connection with God that may be done silently, verbally, privately, or in a group.

During prayer, we may ask assistance from God by focusing our mind upon the positive energy that is God. In a sense, prayer is a means of union with God. When we pray *for* someone, we are asking God to bestow energy upon the person who is the object of our prayer. It does not matter if that person is in the physical world or on the Other Side. Prayers help a spirit on the Other Side by sending them positive energy.

When a person prays for a spirit on the Other Side, the spirit "hears" it. From what spirits have indicated to me, it is like hearing a radio in the background. In a sense, this draws the spirit to the person praying. The spirit may adjust his or her frequency to align with that of the person praying. It is something like a spiritual phone call. Intense emotional feelings by the bereaved may also draw the spirit to the person who is expressing those emotions on the spirit's behalf.

To illustrate, I was attending a psychic development class and a spirit associated with Olivia, one of the students, kept trying to get my attention. During a break, I asked Olivia if I could have a word with her. She was happy to oblige.

I described to her that I saw a young man in a black suit, white shirt, and black tie. He wore his brown hair in a shoulder-length style and appeared to be around sixteen years old. Olivia told me her nephew had recently died in a tragic accident. She confirmed that he was sixteen and that my description fit. "Those were the clothes he was buried in. It was the only time he ever wore a tie," Olivia said. "We were very close. I was his favorite aunt."

"He feels your pain and wants to give you a gift," I conveyed.

"How?" she asked.

"He is showing me an image of himself standing in the middle of a giant bright yellow sunflower. The petals of the sunflower are brilliant and radiate all around the image of the young man."

She paused, a sad look on her face, and said, "The sunflower is my favorite flower." After a few moments, Olivia smiled again. "I hope this means he's ascended to Heaven."

ULTIMATELY, I BELIEVE all spirits will ascend to the higher frequencies of the Other Side. It may take longer for some spirits than it does for others, and the reason may be beyond our comprehension. Spirits remain linked to us, particularly when there was a love connection between them and us. Excessive grieving for a loved one can, in a sense, anchor them to us. They feel our emotions and hear our words and prayers. They are aware of what is going on in our lives, they are concerned about us, and when they feel the pain of a broken heart, they will reach out to comfort us.

A relationship with someone we love never ceases to exist. When the body dies, the immortal spirit lives on and evolves, ascending higher into the Light. Likewise, our relationship with someone in spirit evolves. It transforms from a physical one to one of a purely spiritual nature. We are always connected to those we love; love is an immortal force that transcends physical life, time, and space.

Mediumship won't bring someone physically back to earth, but it lets us reach out to communicate with a soul on the Other Side, giving us a glimpse of where that person is now, and it reaffirms that eventually we will be reunited.

After all, we are just living in the material world for now.

7

How to Reach Out
to the Other Side

A loved one has passed, and you believe
it will help you cope with your grief
to make contact with the spirit of that person. You
may ask yourself these questions: When am I ready
for a reading? Is there a period of time I need to
wait before going for a reading? If I'm ready to
engage in spirit contact, how do I go about choosing a medium?

Many people want to make contact immediately after a loved one has passed, when they are traumatized and in shock. To them, accepting the reality of the situation seems impossible. This leads to their intense desire to find and hold on to their loved one at any cost. Realistically, is this the best time for the person here in the material world to make contact with the Other Side?

Spirits can communicate immediately after transitioning to the Other Side, and sometimes they do. It has happened a lot in my family. I've also encountered numerous people who have told me about the appearance of a loved one's spirit right after that person physically died.

An intriguing example of a spirit communicating just after a passing occurred during a reading for Alicia. An uncle's spirit appeared, although at first I wasn't sure that he was related to her. Alicia has blond hair, blue eyes, and a very fair complexion. This man had a distinctly Middle Eastern appearance.

I described him, and Alicia looked somewhat surprised. "My husband is from the Middle East—that's his uncle Jafar."

"Uncle Jafar says he feels great now and is happy to be rid of his body," I relayed. "He was tired of having tubes up his nose and in his arms. Breathing was labored for him, and he hated the painful lesions on his legs and feet. The odd thing, Alicia, is that it seems like he hasn't been on the Other Side very long."

"Uncle Jafar was very ill for a long time." Alicia paused. "He died four hours ago."

"That's terrible," I said. "We can reschedule your reading if this is too much."

"No, I'm fine; please go on," Alicia replied.

"Well," I continued, "Uncle Jafar agrees—in fact, he is insistent about communicating."

"Uncle Jafar was all business and always got right to the point," Alicia explained.

"This is unusual," I commented. "I know this will sound weird, but here goes: he's standing on the deck of an ancient and luxurious golden boat. He's surrounded by art and treasure; it looks to me like Cleopatra's barge!"

"Mark Anthony sees Cleopatra's barge? Now that *is* interesting," Alicia said with a slight smile.

"I told you it was unusual," I replied as the Mark Antony and Cleopatra association dawned on me.

"This does make sense, though," Alicia explained. "Uncle Jafar wasn't Egyptian, but he was royalty. He was a member of a Middle Eastern royal family. They were forced to flee their country because of a revolution. And he did like big, expensive yachts!"

Uncle Jafar's message continued. "He loves his family very much. He thanks his wife for always staying by his side. He asks his son to lead the family with courage, and he wants his daughter to know he was always proud of her strength and wisdom," I conveyed.

Alicia smiled. "Family meant everything to him. They'll be relieved to hear his message."

While Jafar's spirit felt his family needed to hear from him right away, sometimes spirits do not communicate immediately, and they seem to have their reasons for this. The survivors may not be emotionally ready for the contact right after their loss. There is no instant cure for grief; it is an ongoing healing process. Mediumship can be part of the healing process; however, it must come at the appropriate time, and that depends on the individual. For most, it may take some months to process the initial shock and trauma before they can receive the full benefit of any messages from the Other Side. For others, it may take years before they are emotionally ready. This is why most mediums recommend allowing emotional stability and a sense of normalcy to return before you consult with a medium.

THE OBJECTIVE OF mediumship is to prove the continuation of life after physical death and the immortal nature of the soul. It can also be a means of resolving lingering emotional issues with the person who died. However, mediumistic contact with the Other Side may not be for everyone.

I have a friend whose father died. Four years after his passing, my friend was still angry at his father for being an alcoholic and abusive parent. Based on what he'd told me over the years, he carried a lot of unresolved issues. I offered to conduct a reading for him and was surprised when he asked, "Will it take long? I'm trying to get a tee time for golf that day."

Instead of trying to convince him that this might be healing for him, I just let it go. Some people are open to spirit
contact; others are not. It is also true that some may never be
ready. However, this is a good friend, so I left the door open
in the event he decides he wants to resolve his anger. It is
entirely his decision, and it is totally inappropriate to try to
impose a reading on someone.

FOR A PERSON who does want a reading, finding the right
medium is important. Some mediums may feel more suitable
to you than others. It is a lot like finding the right attorney to
handle your case. You should do your research and check his
or her qualifications and experience. The medium may have a
website, and if so, you should read it.

If possible, talk to other people who have received a reading from that medium. Prior to the reading, you will most
likely have the opportunity to talk with the medium on the
telephone or in person. Find out what the reading will cost
and ask how he or she works—by this, I mean find out how
the session is conducted, as well as how the medium receives
information. It helps to have an idea of what to expect.

It is advisable to give the medium very little information
about the person you hope to contact prior to the reading.
For example, my policy is to request that people not tell me
anything in advance about themselves or the individual with
whom they wish to connect. This isn't always feasible. While
I understand the desire to communicate with a specific spirit,

I ask them not to give me any additional details. My philosophy is that the contact must be legitimate and not tainted by anything I have been told.

Based on my own experiences, mediumship is a blessing. For me, once the door to the Other Side opened, there was no turning back. Accepting and embracing my inherited ability changed my life completely. Not only has spirit contact helped me to heal from my own grief, it has brought a means of assisting others in their healing processes.

Mediumship is a "service gift" to be used in the service of others. I feel it is a great honor to touch people's lives in such a manner. Mediumship is also a tremendous responsibility, which must be approached with reverence and humility. Although it has been and is still the greatest challenge of my life, it is also a responsibility I thank God for every day.

For the medium, every reading is a spiritual test. The test is to give the best reading you can. The bereaved need and deserve this. They are devastated and filled with doubt, fear, and pain. They are seeking a connection to determine whether a loved one continues to exist. There may be several emotional issues that need resolution. A mediumistic reading can be a major step in the healing process. So, when a grief-stricken individual seeks the assistance of a medium, it is the medium's obligation to do everything possible to facilitate the most powerful connection possible with the Other Side.

Ordinarily, the medium is just one of three components involved in a reading, the other two being the client (the person seeking the reading) and the spirit. However, it is not unusual for more than one spirit to communicate, so there could be more than three individuals involved.

If the client is spiritually open and receptive, it is easier for the medium to make a connection. It is the client who draws the spirit to the medium, not the other way around. The medium receives the information from the spirit and conveys it to the client.

When you go to a medium for a reading, it is natural to be excited and a bit nervous. You may want to bring along a list of questions, or you may hope to hear from a specific person or persons. This is not always the best approach. It might be better to go into the reading with no expectations and allow the information that comes through the medium to flow. It has been my experience that the spirits who connect will know what needs to be communicated.

Try to schedule the reading so it will be the only major thing you do that day. Squeezing a reading in on your lunch hour or between plans with friends isn't always a good idea. If you can, take the day off. You will want some time to process and assimilate the information and messages received. It often takes time to recognize the relevance of what a spirit conveys.

I believe it is important to focus on the love of God and on the pure energy of God's white light when engaging in spirit contact. It must also be done with the highest of intentions. For me, the best way to do this is to pray. In fact, I pray before all readings, interviews, and public appearances.

It is my belief that prayer raises vibrational frequency and keeps the spiritual atmosphere of the reading positive. In my opinion, the denomination of the prayers doesn't matter as long as you connect with God. Since I was raised as a Catholic and am most familiar with Catholic prayers, I say the rosary prior to a reading. A rosary is a circle of prayer beads designed to allow one to pray without distraction.

Then, when I meet with the client, I like to say a few additional prayers with that person before we begin. I am not seeking to convert anyone to any particular religion, and I do not wish to impose my beliefs upon anyone. This is simply my method of charging the area with positive energy and setting the tone. I ask God to permit only spirits of the highest of purposes to come into the vibration of the person receiving the reading. I believe this keeps negative energy away.

Not all mediums use my methodology. I have studied extensively with mediums from all over the world, and many have different approaches. It is fascinating to see how my colleagues from different countries and different faiths do things. However, we all ask God for assistance and guidance. I have yet to meet a medium who doesn't believe in a higher power.

SOME INDIVIDUALS MAY wish to initiate contact with the Other Side on their own. This may be possible, because each of us is capable of having a mediumistic experience. It can be frustrating, however, since not everyone is able to carry on coherent communication with a discarnate intelligence. That is why some people use a Ouija board or another device to assist in their attempts to connect with the Other Side.

I am often asked if Ouija boards are evil. In and of them-selves, Ouija boards are not evil. They are pieces of wood—inanimate objects. By analogy, a loaded gun is also an inani-mate object. A gun is not evil, yet anyone who would give a loaded gun to a young child is obviously not acting with the best intentions and is certainly not comprehending the potential repercussions.

It is the intention of the person using the device and how it is used that determine if it will be a conduit for negative energy. Often purchased in toy stores and therefore perceived as a novelty, a Ouija board might be used by a gathering of people who have a few glasses of wine and play with it: "Let's see who we can conjure up!" No protective prayers are said; no one invokes the guidance of God's white light. This illustrates how a Ouija board might be used for less than the highest of purposes.

When there is no logic or intelligence associated with the activity, you may get negative results. Legitimate medi-ums understand the difference between spirit contact and the manipulation of the subconscious mind. Mediumship is dif-ferent from the power of the mind, which can manipulate the Ouija board. Mediums know when messages are from spirits and not merely part of a parlor game.

Spirit contact is not entertainment and should never be treated as such. It is a serious activity and should be approached with dignity, love, and respect. Drinking alcohol and laughing over a board game will not necessarily attract positive spiritual energies. By analogy, it is like throwing a cast net into the spirit world and hoping to catch Flipper—but catching Jaws instead. Do not voluntarily engage in spirit contact unless you are properly prepared and protected.

A legitimate medium possesses the natural skills for spirit contact and will not require something like a Ouija board to open the door to the Other Side. They themselves do not conjure up or summon any particular spirit or spirits. A loved one on the Other Side who needs to communicate with someone here will do so. The client is the one that "brings" a spirit to the reading, not the medium. The medium is the conduit.

Trust in God's guidance is essential. When a spirit communicates information, which the medium translates as symbols or images, one must believe in its significance. What may be thought of as an irrelevant detail may be an extremely important message or piece of validation from a spirit. Spirits are not wrong. What may be inaccurate is the medium's or client's interpretation or misinterpretation of what is being received—or the failure on the medium's part to convey an important detail.

Small details can be extremely relevant. For example, I was conducting a reading for Marybeth when I received a clairaudient message that sounded like a young man saying "Follow the yellow brick road."

I repeated this phrase to Marybeth. She laughed out loud and said, "Oh my God, that is Larry! He was totally into Judy Garland. His favorite movie was *The Wizard of Oz*. Whenever things were going badly for me, he would tell me that to cheer me up." Although I remember the movie, this particular phrase was not significant to me; however, it meant a lot to her. Clairaudient messages are often concise and quite profound.

DURING A READING for Marion, her father came through and sent her a lot of positive messages. She was happy to make a connection with him, as they had been close. He projected a lot of information about Marion's childhood and their father-daughter relationship. Among these large details and vivid memories, I saw the image of a small piece of jewelry. This particular item didn't seem too unusual or unique, so I almost ignored it. Nevertheless, I am obliged to convey what I am given, so I told her, "He is showing me a small heart-shaped locket. It is silver in color and on a silver chain."

Marion's eyes opened wide. Apparently, her father's spirit wanted me to describe the locket, which at first I'd deemed trivial.

She said, "My father gave that locket to me years ago. Ever since he died, I keep a fragment of his ashes in it."

I had trusted in the information presented by her father's spirit, and this turned out to be a significant part of the subsequent message from him.

Once she acknowledged the locket, I heard a clairaudient message, which I relayed: "Let go. Let them go. Let my ashes go."

Obviously, he meant for her to release his ashes.

Solemnly she admitted, "It's been four years since he died, and I've never fully accepted his passing. I just can't let go of him. I keep the urn with his ashes in the living room. I miss him so much, but I am realizing now that I'll never really be at peace until I spread his ashes."

Marion needed the physical release of her father's ashes to facilitate the emotional acceptance of his passing. She closed her eyes and took a few deep breaths as we sat in silence. Then she said, "Thank you for helping me to understand this."

"I appreciate that," I replied. "However, first thank God, and then thank your father's spirit, because he's the one who sent you the message."

I MET LANA briefly at a lecture I'd given on life after death. She told me she was grieving the loss of her daughter and would like a reading. I agreed but asked that she not tell me anything else. Two weeks later, she came to see me.

During the reading, I described what appeared to be her daughter's spirit. Lana confirmed the description and then said, "Mr. Anthony, I know that many people feel a loved one around, yet ever since my daughter, Betsy, died, I haven't felt her presence around me at all."

"Betsy transmitted information that I perceive as images of Halloween and Christmas," I said, "with lots of decorations, pumpkins, and Christmas trees."

"Since she passed, I dread the holidays," Lana explained. "It is just so hard, because it brings back so many painful memories."

"Lana, I keep seeing another image repeated over and over," I conveyed.

"What is it?" she asked.

"I see a crystal or glass angel being placed on a Christmas tree. In fact, it looks like you are the one putting the angel on the tree," I explained.

Lana gasped when I mentioned this.

"I'm sorry, I don't mean to upset you, but I have to describe accurately what I'm receiving."

"No, it's not upsetting at all," Lana said excitedly. "It's just that I can't believe you said that about me putting a crystal angel on the Christmas tree."

"She is insistent about this image," I responded. "This image keeps getting repeated."

"The other day I was thinking about Christmas and how sad it was going to be without her again. Then, all of a sudden, this idea popped into my head that I needed to put up a Christmas tree and, I can't believe this, decorate it with crystal and glass angels. I like angels, but I never thought to put only angels, especially glass ones, on the Christmas tree," Lana said.

"Who do you think gave you that idea?" I asked.

Lana stared at me. Her expression turned from sadness to one of joy as she cried, "Betsy!"

"Now I'm seeing a radio, and you are turning the knob on the radio," I described.

"Oh my! I can't believe I didn't notice this before!" Lana said excitedly. "Many times, I will turn on the radio for no reason at all—and then a song plays that reminds me of Betsy!"

I started to chuckle. "Betsy seemed to be a very happy and loving person."

"Oh, she was!" Lana replied.

"Betsy has another message: 'Do you still think I'm not with you?'" I conveyed.

Now it was Lana who lit up like a Christmas tree. "She is, isn't she? I guess I wasn't paying attention—or didn't know what to look for."

"Spirit contact can be very subtle," I explained. "A spirit will plant suggestions, send you images or sometimes verbal messages, or present feelings. Betsy wants you to know she's been around you a lot."

"Oh, thank you! I feel so much better," Lana said with a beaming smile. "Without you, I never would have realized this."

"In this case, pun intended, I was the radio. All I did was tune in to the Other Side and deliver her message," I explained.

SINCE SPIRITS ARE eternal beings, their perception of time is much different than time as we know it. What we perceive as a long time may just be a few moments by their reckoning. That being the case, the questions remain: When will someone be ready for a reading? How long before a spirit contacts someone here in the material world? The answers may just be with the spirits on the Other Side, as Bridgett came to realize.

I was having dinner at a pizzeria one evening with a group of friends. They were asking me questions about what it was like to be a medium and about the nature of spirit contact. During our conversation, one of my friends, Bridgett, said, "I wonder why I've never heard from my husband, Dave. It's been seventeen years since he died, and I've tried so hard to get him to visit me from the Other Side. He never comes through."

This surprised me, because Bridgett is a very spiritual person who attends many classes on psychic development, religion, and spirituality. If anyone should be receptive to spirit contact, she should.

Suddenly, I felt a tingling sensation along the back of my spine coupled with a sense of heightened awareness, which means a spirit is trying to make contact with me.

"Pancakes," I blurted out.

"What did you say?" Bridgett asked, astonished.

"He liked pancakes," I replied, "and he is showing me an orange traffic cone. Does that make sense to you?"

"Dave loved pancakes for breakfast," Bridgett said excitedly. "He was a firefighter, and he always kept those orange traffic cones in the garage."

"I'm sorry, Bridgett. This really isn't the appropriate time or place for a reading. For goodness' sake, we're in a pizzeria!" I explained.

"Please," she implored. "It is the perfect time and place. I'm surrounded by all my friends."

"Okay," I said, returning my attention to Dave's spirit. "He was a big guy, and he had a lot of health problems. It feels like tumors all over his body. I believe he died of cancer."

"He did die of cancer," she said, now looking very sad.

"He wants you to know that living in the house near the beach with the white wooden stairs leading up to the front door was the happiest time of his life," I conveyed.

"That was our house," she said, "and it was also the house he died in." After a thoughtful pause, she asked, "Did I do enough for him?"

"He wants you to know no one could've done more. He'd like it if you would stop beating yourself up. He also feels that you have a lot of patience with everyone but yourself," I relayed.

"Sounds like Dave," she said with a brief smile. "I've always felt guilty that I didn't do enough."

"You were there when he made the transition. You made it easier. You held his hand. He thanks you for that and loves you very much."

"He died at three o'clock in the morning," Bridgett acknowledged. "He lapsed into a coma. Thank you. I needed to hear that he knew I held his hand when he died."

"He knows that after his passing, you totally fell apart," I told her. "You were thinking very dark thoughts for about three months."

Bridgett's bright eyes grew wide. "He knows that?"

"He says it was your mother, who is still here in the material world, who intervened and told you to get ahold of yourself. He also says that was the only time he and his mother-in-law ever agreed on anything."

Although tears were streaming from her eyes, Bridgett started to laugh. "He and my mother couldn't stand each other, but that makes total sense. They both always loved me."

Then Bridgett asked, "Why has it taken seventeen years for him to contact me?"

"His response is this: 'It was time. You were not ready then. You are ready now.'"

8

Rescuing Spirits—
Sometimes They Need Our Help

$\mathcal{S}$pirits come to the rescue of the bereaved by communicating with us and helping us through our grief. Sometimes, though, it seems as if it is the spirits who need our help in transitioning to the Light of the Other Side. This "spirit rescue" involves helping spirits who have not let go of the material world and who still linger here. Coming to the rescue of a spirit and knowing you have helped a loved one in spirit can be very healing for those of us in the material world and for spirits on the Other Side.

These spirits are commonly referred to as ghosts. In addition to my own work and experiences, I've consulted with several mediums and paranormal investigators regarding this type of spectral phenomenon. There are different schools of thought on the nature of these entities. While the phenomenon has been the subject of innumerable books, television shows, and movies, I address ghosts only in the context of healing. Healing is a two-way street—they can help us and, at times, we can help them. It is a wonderful feeling for those here in the material world to know that through our love, we can in some way help a spirit transition into the peace and beauty of the Light.

One school of thought is that once we die, we immediately go to the Other Side and do not linger here. Since we are spirits having a material-world experience, when we die we separate from the physical body and then return to our natural state as an immortal living spirit. That being the case, what we perceive as a ghost is not a spiritual entity at all but instead a vibration related to an event.

This theory asserts that physical matter retains vibration. So, in the case of a death, particularly one of a traumatic nature, the physical matter holds the energy of this event. Physical matter can include an object or the place where the event occurred. This energetic vibration replays continuously, much like an echo. This means that a ghost is no more a living spirit than a reflection in a mirror is a living person.

People detect this vibratory echo and perceive it as a ghostly presence. This accounts for hauntings. I understand it is possible to interrupt this echo, thereby terminating its constant refrain and ending the so-called haunting.

Another school of thought is also predicated on the fact that we are all immortal spirits temporarily housed in a human body. When the body dies, a person separates from the physical body and—as an intelligent, immortal living spirit—has a choice as to what happens next. This choice involves whether to transition to the Other Side or to refuse to let go of the material world. In a sense, the spirit is "trapped," albeit by choice, between the material world and the Other Side.

The spirit has the option of acknowledging that he or she is between two worlds and can voluntarily let go and enter the Light. A good (if somewhat dramatic) example of this is the last scene in the movie *Ghost*. In that scene, Patrick Swayze's character fulfills his mission here on the physical side of existence and then ascends into the Light. This is Hollywood at its most theatrical but is a great example nonetheless.

Assisting or directing a spirit to ascend into the Light is known as "spirit rescue." It is my opinion that, for various reasons, certain spirits do not always go directly into the Light; usually, it is those individuals who died suddenly or traumatically who do not. Sometimes there may be an unresolved issue in the material world that causes the spirit to linger. Without realizing that he or she is dead—or acknowledging death but being afraid to let go—the spirit lingers between the material world and the Other Side.

This uncertain state—when a spirit does not let go—may account for what is known as a haunting. Instead of being afraid of these spirits, we must understand that they need our help. They must be directed to release the fear or the attachment to this plane and ascend into the Light.

LaWanda called me on the telephone to ask about strange events that were occurring in her home. "Mr. Anthony," she said, "I hope you can help me. I think my house is haunted."

She definitely had my interest. "Please tell me what's happening."

"My friends and family say they don't believe me. They think I might be crazy, but they're scared too. And now they've stopped coming over to my house because of whatever this thing is," she explained.

"What do you think it is?" I asked.

"Every time I come home, I feel these cold chills running up and down the back of my spine. Then I feel like someone is watching me. I've tried to ignore him, but he doesn't go away."

"You said 'him.' Why do you think this entity is male?" I asked.

"My two-year-old keeps saying something about seeing this man—and I'm afraid she is going to be possessed by the devil!"

"Hold on," I told her. "Why do you think this male presence is evil?"

"Well, whatever he is, I get chills, and that frightens me— and I don't like the fact that my little girl can see him," she said excitedly.

"Spirits are energy, and when a spirit's energetic field interfaces with our energy, we receive electrical impulses, which we experience as cold chills. This sensation is interpreted as fear because, physiologically, it is the same sensation we experience when we are afraid," I told her. "The spiritual presence may not really be negative at all. He may just be trying to communicate with you."

"What about my baby? Why is this thing talking to her?"

"Children are very open psychically. They can often perceive spirits; that is not unusual. As we grow up, we are taught to disregard things other people can't see," I explained. "I don't think that is a negative thing. You never know, your daughter might be a medium."

"Lord Almighty! What next?" LaWanda's voice expressed her concern.

Since she was halfway across the country and it wasn't practical for me to make a house call, I asked LaWanda if she would mind if I conducted a reading over the telephone to see who might be around her spiritually.

"If you think that will help, then please do whatever you can," LaWanda said.

Immediately, the spirit of a man wanted to communicate. He wasn't a negative energy at all. "There is an older gentleman's spirit around you. He died suddenly of a heart attack," I explained.

"You can see him? What does he look like?" LaWanda wanted to know.

"He is African-American, and since I watch a lot of TV," I explained, "this may sound corny, but do you remember the show *The Jeffersons*?"

"Yes," she said slowly.

"Well, this spirit looks kind of like the actor who played George Jefferson," I said.

"You've got to be kidding me!" LaWanda cried, sounding outraged.

"I'm sorry," I apologized. "I didn't mean to be offensive—"

"No, that's not it at all! My father looked like George Jefferson—we used to tease him about it. Are you telling me that Daddy is haunting my house? Why in the world would he do that?" LaWanda asked. "Is he mad because we teased him about looking like George Jefferson?"

"His message is that he is proud of you and your little girl. He is excited about the granddaughter he never got to meet when he was here," I conveyed. "That's why he talks to her now."

"He died of congestive heart failure about a year before she was born," LaWanda told me. "I miss Daddy so much. I always felt bad that he never got to know my daughter. And you're saying *he* is the one talking to her, not some evil spirit?"

"No, he isn't negative at all. He's a proud grandfather. He doesn't want to scare you and apologizes if his presence has upset you. He wants you to know how much he loves you and his granddaughter. He didn't get the chance to say good-bye, and he regrets that he never got to meet his granddaughter."

"Oh, Daddy!" LaWanda exclaimed. "How I wish I could've said goodbye to you! Tell him I love him so much, and I miss him terribly."

"He says he knows that already, because you were his baby girl. And now that he's made contact, it's time for him to move on."

"Does he really have to go?" LaWanda asked. "Now that I know it's him, I feel better. I don't need to be scared any-more."

"He says it is time for him to let go, but he'll be around," I relayed.

"This helps a lot," LaWanda told me. "I love knowing that Daddy is still looking out for me."

THIS READING BROUGHT back memories of how frighten-ing spirit contact can be when you don't fully understand it. I may have been born a medium, but that doesn't mean I've always known how to fully understand or control my ability.

I recall a student trip to Germany I took in the summer of 1979. Along with a group of fellow students—including a childhood friend, Dave—I visited the Dachau concentra-tion camp near Munich. A history buff, I had an interest in

World War II and figured this would be a fascinating learning experience. Dachau was one of the first Nazi death camps established for the extermination of Jews and other "enemies of the state" under Hitler's regime. After its liberation by Allied Forces near the end of World War II, it has been kept intact as a memorial to the nearly 40,000 people who perished there—a remembrance so that what happened there can never happen again.

About a dozen students were on the train from Munich to Dachau. We were laughing about the prior evening at the Hofbräuhaus, a famous beer hall. I mimicked a German accent while telling a funny story about how the woman serving us reminded me of a character out of the TV show *Hogan's Heroes*.

When we got off the train, we took a taxi to the concentration camp's entrance, still joking about the night before. However, as I entered Dachau, for me, the laughter stopped. Fear engulfed me. I tried to shrug it off and concentrate on the historical significance of the place by taking notes and reading the plaques explaining different aspects of the camp.

Dave noticed something was wrong. I must have looked pale. "Hey, buddy, are you all right?"

"Sure, no problem," I replied, trying to look nonchalant. Yet I was not all right. I saw images of starving inmates wearing black-and-white striped camp garb. I felt surrounded by emaciated, anguished faces, their eyes glazed in terror, their arms reaching out to me. I tried to ignore them, thinking my imagination was running rampant.

"Hey, Mark! Check out the gas chamber," Dave said excitedly. "It's even creepier than the pictures in history books!"

"No, thanks, Dave. I'll just wait out here," I replied, unable to even approach this chamber of death where so many forgotten lives had been so callously extinguished. The roar of thousands of agonized voices exploded inside my skull. Trembling, I sat down on the ground, put my hands over my face, and tried not to vomit.

The other students couldn't understand what was happening and were giving me strange looks. I heard one of them say, "What's up with Anthony? He looks like he's freaking out or something."

"Too much partying last night," Dave joked as he walked over to me. He'd known me a long time and knew something really was wrong.

"I can't handle this place!" I whispered, trying to maintain my composure.

Dave grabbed me by the arm, pulled me to my feet, and said, "We have to get Mark back on the train. Besides, I'm over this place, too. It's a downer."

"Thanks, Dave," I said as we left.

"No worries, buddy." Dave smiled. "Maybe you just need a beer."

"More like two," I joked, feeling relieved. I wanted to put as much distance between myself and Dachau as humanly possible.

There was another eerie experience I had a few years later during law school in Macon, Georgia, where my first apartment was in a red brick, five-story building in the historic district. Built in the late 1800s, it had a distinctive Old South charm. I selected this building because it was within walking distance of Mercer Law School. I liked that it was surrounded by flowering dogwood, magnolia, and poplar trees. My basement apartment seemed just the right size for a single law student.

When my parents helped me move in, my mother did not like the place. I figured she didn't like the fact that I was living in a basement apartment. When it came time to say good-bye for the return trip to Florida, Mom said, "I don't want you living in that place. There's darkness there." She had tears in her eyes.

I tried to shrug off her obvious concern.

However, after my parents left, strange things started to happen. Whenever I was in my apartment, I sank into the deepest depression. I experienced tightness around my neck and felt as if I wanted to hang myself. That really threw me for a loop, no pun intended. Overall, I'm a pretty upbeat person and don't believe in suicide. Even if I did, hanging would not be a consideration.

That wasn't all. I was awakened on Friday mornings at 6 AM by the sound of knocking at the door, yet no one was there. The front door buzzer would go off, and no one was there. The phone would ring; no one was on the line. These things happened every Friday at precisely 6 AM. I began to feel darker and darker—that my life was pointless and that there'd never be any joy in my life. I could not sleep peacefully. My dreams faded into nightmares wherein I saw a young man hanging from a noose. Thoughts of hanging myself invaded my mind. This basement apartment was the creepiest place I had ever lived.

What could I do? Even a first-year law student understood that leases do not have a haunted house escape clause.

Then it dawned on me. Only one person would understand something like this: Mom. I called home and told her about all of these negative feelings.

She said, "I know exactly what you mean. I, too, had an eerie feeling about the place. It felt gloomy and filled with darkness. There is a negative presence there. Get out of that place. Break the lease, no matter what it costs."

That was all the validation I needed. I immediately went to the property manager to give her notice.

The property manager was a thin woman in her fifties who looked tired beyond her years. She lived in a second-floor apartment in the same building. She looked me up and down and said in the sweetest Georgia accent, "You are the law student who lives in the, uh, basement apartment, aren't you, sugar?"

"Yes," I replied nervously, "and I really don't like it there."

The smile faded from her face. "Oh dear; I understand. Well, no use in fretting over burnt bacon, is there?"

I wondered what incinerated breakfast food had to do with anything but decided to go with the flow. It sounded like she was going to let me break the lease.

"You can move out today, sugar. We even have another apartment available in a building across the street," she said softly.

"Great!" I almost shouted. Then, trying to hide my enthusiasm, I said coolly, "Well, I guess I'll take it."

She nodded in agreement and though her mouth was smiling, her eyes were not.

Back in my apartment, I packed quickly, before the manager could change her mind. While I was loading everything into my van, I wondered why there had been no questions asked about why I didn't like the apartment. She didn't require a new security deposit, and she didn't have any problem with my leaving immediately. It was as if my request to get out of that dismal place had been expected.

I moved out later that day. As soon as I walked into my new apartment, I experienced a great sense of relief. It felt like the sun had risen in my soul. All suicidal ideation and nightmare scenes stopped; I've never had any like them since.

However, the new apartment, also in an old building, seemed to have a different kind of spiritual presence lingering there. This one seemed to be very playful. My suspicions about that were confirmed when small objects began to fly off the table now and again.

Oh no, not again! Is somebody trying to tell me something?

Yet this presence felt totally different. I had none of the feelings of foreboding I'd experienced in the other apartment. And I wasn't the only one who felt this playful presence.

One night I was talking with one of my neighbors, another law student. We'd had a few beers, so I felt comfortable asking her, "Have you ever thought that the building we live in might be—"

"Haunted?" She finished my sentence. "Totally, but it isn't scary, just freaky."

I got used to the presence and was so busy with my law school homework, I finally just ignored it. Besides, I had grown up with a mother who saw spirits. At least this spirit didn't make me feel like hanging myself.

Looking back, I wonder if those tragic souls at Dachau or the young man's spirit in the basement in Macon, Georgia, were trapped between this world and the Other Side. Were the spirits at Dachau actually spirits, or were they just echoes of the residual vibration of the negative events that occurred there? I hope for the latter. If spirits at places where terrible atrocities have occurred are still lingering there, they need to be directed to let go of this world and to move on into the Light.

In retrospect, I don't believe the spirit in Macon was trying to get me to commit suicide at all. It appears he wanted to be acknowledged or needed help to realize that he was actually physically dead and it was time to go to the Light. Spirits will often transmit information in the form of feelings, including how they felt when they died, in order to verify their identities. I now believe this was the case with this spirit. When I lived in Macon, I didn't understand that. I pray that his soul has since ascended.

These two events always come to mind when I am asked to engage in spirit rescue. Just because a place seems haunted does not mean someone should jump to the conclusion that the spirits are negative.

THE MANAGER OF a department store contacted me and asked if I would investigate an unusual series of events that were taking place. The store sold arts and crafts supplies, and one section of the store had been making the employees extremely uncomfortable.

"Something's not right in the woodworking section," the manager reported. "My employees keep seeing shadows and hearing voices like whispers. They also talk about experiencing cold chills. It's creepy."

"I can't promise anything, but I'll have a look," I told him.

I decided to walk around the store. I didn't feel much of anything until I entered the woodworking section. Then I saw him.

The spirit of a man stood at the far end of the aisle I had just entered. He looked like he was from the 1970s, given his hairstyle and long sideburns. I perceived he was wearing a flannel shirt and blue jeans, carrying a tool belt, and wearing a hard hat—the type construction workers wear. It appeared to me that he was a carpenter or construction worker who might have been killed suddenly in an accident when this store was built. It made sense that he lingered in the woodworking section because this was a familiar environment.

He realized I could see him and, in a flash, he came right up to me. I was surprised at how quickly he moved.

The spirit asked, "Why can't anyone see me?"

This spirit certainly appeared to be a lot more than a residual vibration of a traumatic event. He was asking a coherent question.

"You have died," I replied. "You have to let go."

"I'm afraid," he responded.

"Don't be. You must go into the Light. You will be safe there. You will be surrounded by loved ones, family, friends, and best of all, God," I communicated. Silently, I said a few prayers asking God to send angels to escort him safely into the Light for his own good.

His image faded from my view.

When I told the manager what I'd experienced, he asked, "That's it? Don't you have to burn candles or chant or something?"

"No, I don't believe I do," I said, smiling. I wished him a good night and left.

About a month later, I received a call from the manager. "I don't know what you did, but whatever it was, it worked," he said.

"What do you mean?" I asked.

"No shadows, no voices, no cold chills," he explained. "Best of all, the employees aren't creeped out by the woodworking department anymore."

"I'd like to know when the store was built," I asked.

"Not sure exactly," the manager replied. "Sometime in the 1970s."

IN DECEMBER OF 2007, I had just returned from court. As I walked into my office, my assistant, Lynn, was in tears. "My husband just witnessed a murder!" She was terrified.

Her husband, Kevin, who worked for a moving company, had been loading a van in an upscale neighborhood when the crew heard a commotion at the house next door. A young man ran up the driveway of the house next to where they were working. Another man ran after him, shooting.

Kevin assumed, at first, that they were playing paintball, but then realized that the assailant shot the first man at point-blank range. The victim collapsed on the ground not fifty feet from where Kevin stood. If he wasn't dead, he soon would be; blood was spreading out around his body.

Since I am a criminal defense attorney and this was a murder, I suggested to Lynn that we go to the scene. I knew police would be swarming all over the upper-class neighborhood and we were both concerned for Kevin. Given the location and the circumstances, it was very possible this might have been a contract murder, commonly referred to as a "hit."

Whether it was a hit or not, Kevin was still an eyewitness, so Lynn didn't want her husband's name in the news. In the event the perpetrator was not apprehended, he might decide to hunt down and kill someone that could identify him. We took off in my car. When we arrived, we approached Kevin.

By this time, dozens of law-enforcement officers were working the scene. I nodded to a few I recognized. Unexpectedly, I felt all the hair on the back of my neck stand up. Cold chills covered my body, followed by searing waves of terror. I choked up, feeling nauseous. I realized I was having a contact experience and feeling what the young man had felt in the moments prior to his death. This was a clairsentient experience at its most extreme.

I felt a whir of energy moving immensely fast. It became clear to me that this young man's spirit was racing in circles around and around the property. He seemed to be still running for his life—his life that had ended tragically an hour earlier. It felt like he was in shock, full of fear, and not understanding what had happened. He was disoriented. When he realized that I could see him, his spirit came right up to me.

Lynn saw the look on my face and whispered, "You're doing that *thing* you do, aren't you?"

I nodded. Thankfully, she led her husband and two police officers away from me.

Then I saw his spirit clearly: a young man with a dark complexion, thin, about medium height. He was clean-cut, had black hair parted on the side, and looked Hispanic. I noticed he was wearing olive-drab camouflage clothes.

I walked away to the shade of a large pine tree. The spirit followed me, trying to talk, but his vibration was at such an accelerated level that all I could discern was a high-pitched sound like feedback from a speaker.

I knew I had to do something to help this spirit. He did not realize he was physically dead. Due to the searing waves of fear I felt, it was clear that he had not gone into the Light. I said a quick prayer and reached out to him mentally.

I will never forget the terror in the eyes of this young man's spirit. He looked so pitiful and afraid. "Don't be afraid; you must go into the Light," I told him.

He responded, but I still couldn't understand him. However, I still felt his intense fear.

"If you let go and go into the Light, you will be safe. Friends and family will be waiting for you," I explained. I said another prayer and asked God to send Michael the archangel, Saint Francis, and all of my spirit helpers to escort him safely into the Light.

After I said this prayer, he nodded. His image pixilated, then faded from my view. The waves of fear stopped, and I broke into a cold sweat similar to what happens when a fever breaks. This was followed by a tremendous sigh of relief. I believe he ascended into the Light.

Although I had been sweating profusely and felt emotionally drained from the intensity of the spirit contact, I tried to regain my composure as I walked over to Lynn and Kevin. Despite feeling disheveled, I figured I should act lawyerly now, so I spoke to a police officer and a detective and asked if the victim was a thin, clean-cut Hispanic male about five feet eight, mid-twenties, wearing camouflage-colored clothes. They stopped short and directed their full attention toward me. The police officer stared intently at me as the detective asked, "The body has been secured. How do you know what the victim looked like?"

My sweaty and nervous appearance coupled with my knowledge of the victim made me look suspicious. The police were rapidly concluding I was somehow connected to the crime.

Before I could say anything, Lynn interjected, "My husband told us. He's an eyewitness, and he, uh, told us what the murder victim looked like."

I shot Lynn a thankful glance. She nodded. The police withdrew to question Kevin and the other eyewitnesses.

For mediums, assurance of the accuracy of what we see and experience is always validating. On February 11, 2008, I was at lunch with a friend when I noticed a photo of three men on the front page of the *Florida Today* newspaper. One of them looked surprisingly familiar. I mentioned to my friend, "I know that guy. Who is he?" I figured he might be one of my clients who'd been arrested again, so I bought the paper.

The article was a story about "grow houses." Apparently, drug dealers were using homes in upscale neighborhoods with low crime rates to grow marijuana, so as not to arouse suspicion. The article went on to report that two months ago, on December 11, something went seriously wrong for one family-operated grow house in Melbourne, Florida, resulting in two murders and a suicide. A man went to the grow house, murdered his cousin-in-law, and then drove to a nearby neighborhood where he murdered his brother-in-law before turning the gun on himself. The photos on the front page were of the two murder victims and the perpetrator. Then I realized why one young man looked so familiar. He was the spirit I had encountered at the murder scene.

SOMETIMES, WE'RE THE ones who have to come to the rescue of a spirit by helping the spirit understand that physical life was just a small part of his or her existence. We must communicate to the spirit to let go of the attachment to the material world in order to journey to the next phase of consciousness on the Other Side.

For the person here, part of the journey through grief may be to assist a spirit in letting go and ascending. Based on my experiences, seeing a spirit go to the peace and beauty of the Other Side brings a great sense of relief.

La Wanda found this relief and inner peace when she helped her father's spirit let go of the material world. In her situation, spirit rescue occurred when her father's spirit finally said goodbye after acknowledging his relationship with his granddaughter. It was then that he felt ready to let go. Letting go is important on both sides of existence—here in the material world *and* on the Other Side.

Realizing that a spirit maintains his or her personality, memories, and love is key to accepting the existence of an afterlife. It is healing for someone here to help a spirit move on to the next level of existence. It also helps to bring the understanding that communication with the spirit world is real, enabling us to understand that death is not the end. From beyond the grave, spirits can come to our rescue to teach and to help us resolve lingering issues.

9

Receiving Forgiveness
from the Other Side

*H*ow many times have you wished you could say "I'm sorry" to someone who died? Having regrets about something you did, failed to do, or think you should have done is common. However, such thoughts can intensify your stress and emotional pain, thereby hindering your ability to heal from grief.

Ideally, in life we should treat everyone with love, kindness, and respect. We don't want to wait until someone has died before seeking forgiveness. Of course, that assumes we are always on our best behavior and live in a perfect world. It doesn't take much to see that the material world is far from perfect.

Regrets regarding a deceased loved one arise for a variety of reasons. You may have had an argument where your last words were spoken in anger. Maybe you did something you fear led to the death. You may want to place a lot of blame on the person who died and now feel guilty about that. Personal relationships aren't easy. People can be cantankerous, emotionally distant, self-centered, and downright rude. Even so, that person may die before any issues or arguments between you are resolved. This can leave you with guilt and regrets, wondering what you might have done to change things.

With new and improved capabilities of observation, spirits are aware of the feelings experienced by loved ones here. When possible, they will reach out to try and resolve these issues by forgiving those of us in the material world. The recipient of a message from a spirit may not always understand the contact. Spirits may be all around us, and they do frequently make contact, but these contacts may be subtle.

Sometimes, however, a spirit realizes that subtle contact is not the way to get through and wants to make a more direct connection. This is where a medium can help. At the same time, the recipient of the message from a spirit must be ready and accepting for contact to be transmitted through a medium.

I attended a grief counseling support group at a local church. During the session, I detected the presence of a female spirit near Matilda, one of the attendees. The presence felt like she may have been Matilda's mother. When it came time for Matilda to speak, she shared how much she missed her mother, who had recently passed.

After the meeting, I asked Matilda if I could speak with her.

"You're that medium, aren't you?" she asked.

"Yes. If I can ever be of service to you, please feel free to contact me," I said as I handed her my card.

"How can you help me?" Matilda looked frightened.

"I facilitate communication with spirits who are in Heaven," I explained.

"I don't know about that. That doesn't sound holy," she said, looking nervous.

"If you want, I will leave. I don't want to upset you." It appeared Matilda wasn't prepared for contact with the Other Side.

"Wait! What are you trying to tell me? You know something, don't you?" she asked.

"We can talk some other time. I'm not sure you're ready for this," I explained.

"Tell me. I want to know." Her eyes were full of fear.

"Your mother says that she loves you and is with you often. She is concerned because you have lost your way. She feels you are lost in a forest of despair and can't find your way out. She says your despair makes it so you can't see the forest through the trees."

"Oh my!" She held her hand to her mouth. "That *is* something she would say."

"I'm happy to be of service." I started to walk away.

"Mediums are not of God," she called after me.

Stunned, I turned to look at her. "I believe mediumship is only possible through the grace of God."

"It is the work of Satan!" she stated emphatically.

Mediums constantly have to cope with skeptics and people who are afraid of what they consider the unknown. Instead of being annoyed, I approached the situation like a lawyer. I calmly asked, "Suppose there *is* a devil. Does it want you to believe in God? Does it want you to believe in Heaven? Would it want you to believe your immortal soul lives on after death? Does it want you to know that your loved ones are in the presence of God's White Light? And does it want you to know your loved ones can contact you to let you know they love you and that you will be together again? Do these things sound like satanic objectives?"

"No, I suppose they don't," Matilda agreed.

"I'm only trying to help, and if I offended you in any way, I apologize," I told her.

"What you are doing *is* wrong—it *is* evil." Matilda paused, and then, with a look of embarrassment on her face, quickly added, "But thank you for the beautiful message from my mother!"

SOME PEOPLE THINK that because I'm a medium, I know everything about them or can somehow read their minds. Recently I was introduced to a group of people. One of the men I met said sarcastically, "My name is Richard, but I guess you knew that already."

Although I'm used to comments like that, there is always the temptation to say, "Really, I thought your name was Jerk!"

However, these types of comments and skepticism are part of what comes with the territory. Mediums are not prophets or saints, nor are they all-knowing and all-seeing. Only God is all-knowing and all-seeing. Mediums are human beings, with all of the foibles and imperfections that come with having a material-world existence. We are here to act as the telephone between the material world and the Other Side. This is why I believe that mediumship is a gift from God to be used in the service of others.

Consider the many gifts from God that serve our fellow human beings. They are the parents, doctors, nurses, clergy, teachers, lawyers, plumbers, landscapers, farmers, mechanics, good neighbors, and simply good listeners. A wondrous variety exists among the children of God, and we each have our part to play. Mediumship is just one of the many ways one human being can help another. Anything one can do to assist another person is a gift from God. We are here to help each other, not to harm or exploit one another. Albert Einstein summed it up perfectly: "Only a life lived in the service to others is worth living."

Mediums cannot take away the pain of grief, but they can be a conduit for a spirit to make contact with someone here in the material world. I have been asked why a spirit would want to contact us. In most instances, it is to resolve unfinished business, which often involves the pain of guilt.

DORIS WANTED TO make contact with her husband, Eddie, who had passed twelve years earlier. Doris met with me for a reading. Almost immediately, Eddie came through as a man wearing a yellow golf shirt on a golf course, standing beside a set of clubs. I described the scene to her, along with his physical appearance—even the type of glasses he was wearing. Then Eddie projected the most intense feeling of love for Doris and presented an image of a red Valentine heart—a symbol that I always recognize as love. He came across as such a gentle and loving man, giving me glimpses of the ways he showed his affection for Doris. I explained this to her.

"He was such a romantic—never forgot a birthday or anniversary," she said.

"Eddie says that the two of you were very amorous and had quite an active, how shall I put this, love life," I conveyed.

"Eddie! You stop that!" Doris said, blushing. It was nice to see her smile for a few moments.

Always the gentleman, even on the Other Side, Eddie backed off this particular piece of information. Then he presented me with the image of a shiny red apple. This was not a clairvoyant symbol of any significance to me, so I asked Doris, "Does a shiny red apple have any special meaning for you?"

Doris looked puzzled and said, "I'm not sure. I don't know."

The image became more intense, conveying its importance. I focused intently on this and then heard clairaudiently, "An apple a day keeps the doctor away, but it would've happened anyway." I repeated these words to her.

Doris gasped and said, "Good heavens! We had the biggest argument the morning he died."

"He is acknowledging the argument—that is what is significant about the apple," I relayed.

"Eddie wasn't feeling well, and I made an appointment for him with his doctor. He said, 'I'm not going. I can't stand doctors. I want to play golf, even if it kills me.' Eddie died of a stroke on the golf course two hours later." She looked down, becoming very still.

Then I received another message. "I forgive you. You are released from the guilt."

When Doris heard these words, she covered her mouth with her hands and closed her eyes. After a few moments, she said, "I've been living with this guilt for twelve years. Why did I have to argue with him that morning? We always got along so well except for that one day. I've felt so guilty that our last words were angry ones. I've always wondered if Eddie would be alive today if only I'd been nicer…maybe he would've gone to the doctor."

Since Eddie's death, gnawing guilt had become Doris's constant companion. Eddie was aware she could not forgive herself and was suffering because of it. He came through to tell her that it had been his time to die. It wouldn't have mattered if he had been in a hospital or on the golf course; that was the day. His death wasn't her fault. She couldn't have prevented it.

Much of what we encounter in this life is beyond our control. My personal belief is that there is a time to be born and a time to die. I believe these things are somehow decided prior to our birth. It is what we do between these dates that we have some control over. Many life lessons will be presented to us. How we handle those lessons is what we are in the material world to learn, to accomplish, and to endure.

As a medium, I deliver a message, and then I must let go of the outcome. What happens next is up to the recipient. Whether or not Doris stopped feeling guilty over arguing with Eddie about seeing the doctor is beyond my control. I cannot absolve someone of guilt; however, Eddie's spirit could. He knew how Doris felt, and his spirit made it a point to say he forgave her. In this case, I hope the message gave Doris the impetus to let go of the sorrow and to forgive herself.

THE OLD SAYING "Never judge a book by its cover" certainly applied to Ruth. A redhead with freckles and blue eyes, she dressed conservatively and looked as if she could have been anyone's mom. She entered my office with a smile. Her upbeat personality was extremely pleasant, and it seemed she didn't have a care in the world. I was happy to conduct a reading for her.

During the reading, several of her family members came through. One spirit in particular, her maternal grandfather, encouraged her to stay away from alcohol.

"That's good advice," Ruth smiled. "I hope he knows I've been sober now for four years."

It was clear there was more to Ruth than what was apparent on the surface.

"Another spirit is coming through," I explained. "A young woman: tall, thin, blond, attractive. She's been on the Other Side for some time."

Ruth's demeanor changed dramatically. She became very serious. "Tell me about her."

"Her end was violent. I feel a crushing sensation in my upper throat—an impact right under my chin, almost like a gunshot," I explained.

"That is where she was shot," Ruth said. "I want to know more. That's the reason I came here."

This reading suddenly became extremely intense.

"She wasn't alone when she died. She was with a man," I continued. "He was a physically large man, much bigger than she was."

"What can you tell me about him?" Ruth asked, her gaze locked on mine.

"He was cruel and brutal. That is how she is describing him to me. And, uh…," I paused.

"Go ahead, I can handle it," Ruth said.

"There are piles of white powder—it looks like sugar but isn't sugar," I said, hoping she would understand.

"Cocaine," Ruth said, getting the hint. "What else?"

"She's telling me this was a sex and cocaine deal that went bad, very bad. She says she bit off a bigger piece than she could chew," I explained.

"Makes total sense. This shouldn't have happened," Ruth said. "She was one of my girls. I didn't protect her."

Ruth wasn't your typical next-door neighbor. In her younger days, she had been a high-priced prostitute. Then she had become a madam, and the spirit was that of one of her girls—that is, one of the prostitutes she used to manage.

"She's telling me that he tried to make it look like she committed suicide, but it wasn't suicide—it was murder," I conveyed.

"That's what I always thought," Ruth confided. "The police concluded it was just another depressed, tweaked-out coke whore who shot herself in the head. I knew better. She was smart, and she wasn't the type who'd kill herself. I didn't like it that she got involved in drug deals on the side. What you're telling me makes total sense." With that, Ruth started to sob, "It's been twenty years, and I still feel it's my fault. If only I had stopped her."

"She wants to leave you with a message," I said.

"Please, tell me," Ruth said through the tears.

"She says her death was not your fault."

"That is kind of you to say," Ruth said.

"There's more. She says you'll understand," I explained.

"What?" Ruth asked.

"She's showing me the image of a beautiful yellow butterfly," I relayed.

"For real? She loved yellow butterflies!" Ruth beamed. "Tell her I appreciate that. That means everything to me. This totally validates her message. Oh my God! I feel as if I've been given a new direction in life."

"By the way ...," I started to continue.

"There's something else? What?" Ruth wanted to know.

"She says you really need to stop smoking," I conveyed.

"Wow, I suppose she can see me in the bathroom, too? No, don't tell me," Ruth added.

FOR MANY SPIRITS, it is important to resolve the unfinished business of survivor guilt. I conducted a reading for Benton, who was an interesting man. He was a rancher from Montana in his early thirties. He had come to Florida to get his brother Buckey out of jail. His family of three brothers and two sisters raised beef cattle. In my capacity as an attorney, I represented his brother Buckey. He'd been temporarily incarcerated, but I had been able to get him released. Buckey was the black sheep of the family, the one who always seemed to be in trouble. Benton intended to get Buckey and take him back out West.

While Benton and I were waiting for the time-consuming process of releasing Buckey from jail, I knew I had to talk to Benton.

When a spirit wants to get a message through, the spirit will make its presence known, and one was really working on me to say something to Benton. I must admit, I wasn't sure that this cowboy was the type of person I could talk to about spirit contact, so I was reluctant. But I continued to feel I was being directed to do this, so I took a chance.

I asked Benton, "What do you think about life after death?"

"I was raised to believe in God and in Heaven," he replied.

So far, so good. Then I asked, "What do you think about mediums—people who communicate with spirits?"

He blushed, gave me a double take, and then said, "I do believe there are some people who can talk to spirits. A lot of Indians—I mean Native Americans—believe in that. I've seen some weird stuff out on the range."

A feeling of relief came over me. I was pleasantly surprised when Benton leaned over and whispered, "I feel my father's spirit around me a lot. Sometimes I even smell his pipe tobacco. I can't explain it, but I just know it's him."

Despite having been wrong about Benton, I felt I was in the right place at the right time. "Benton, would you trust me to do a reading for you? I am a medium."

His face brightened. He nodded his head, agreeing enthusiastically.

Benton's father came through. The first impression I had was that his name also started with the letter *B*. I subsequently learned that everyone in this family had a name beginning with *B*.

"I get the sense your father was a real outdoorsman. His spirit is showing me images of mountains, streams, and fishing poles. He's showing me a large brown dog he loved—and a horse."

"Yeah, buddy, keep going," Benton said.

"His personality in life was rigid and strict," I said as Benton stared keenly. "As a father, he was a stern disciplinarian."

When I told Benton this and gave a physical description of the spirit, Benton confirmed that this was his father. "He rode a horse, had that dog, and loved to fish! And, boy, was he ever tough on us."

"Your father was a man's man and, although he didn't show his feelings much in life, he wants his children to know he loved all of you greatly." I conveyed the spirit's message.

"Keep going, sir," Benton said politely.

Clairsentience struck again. "Ooh," I coughed, feeling my lungs filling up. I experienced a short, quick stabbing pain under the sternum. "I sense your father was a heavy smoker, maybe had emphysema. It feels like he died of a heart attack."

Benton nodded. "Yes, sir, on all three counts."

Then I relayed what I heard the spirit say: "'I wouldn't have had it any other way. I wanted to go quickly.'"

"That's Dad, all right. He never would've wanted a long, slow death. He wanted it over, quick and easy," Benton reflected.

"Your father's spirit is deeply concerned about your brother Buckey."

"Everyone in the family is worried about Buckey," Benton stated.

"Your father wants you to tell Buckey to stop drinking and to find a clear direction in his life. It wasn't Buckey's fault that he died," I conveyed.

"Wow, that makes a lot of sense," Benton exclaimed.

"Buckey needs to release the guilt surrounding your father's death," I explained. "This is very important."

"Buckey was working at the ranch and living with Dad when he died," Benton explained. "In fact, Buckey was in the room next to Dad, passed out. It's been years, but Buckey still wonders if Dad called out and he didn't hear because he was drunk as a skunk and out cold. This guilt haunts Buckey night and day." Benton continued, "It's probably no big surprise, but right after Dad died, Buckey drank more heavily. He wanted to drown his guilt. Then he started getting arrested. Buckey's a decent, straightforward guy when he's sober, but when he's drunk, watch out. He starts fights."

Buckey blamed himself for their father's death, but the message from his father was clear. "Your dad was to die that day, and Buckey could not have prevented it," I told Benton.

"Boy, Buckey definitely needs to hear this," Benton said.

The father did not want Buckey to continue to suffer from the survivor guilt over failing to be there to somehow change the outcome.

Benton continued, "Heck yeah—I'll be happy to deliver *this* message to my brother!"

MANY PEOPLE SUFFER with guilt every day, thinking they might have done something to save their loved one's life. Guilt is a companion you can live without; guilt is not your friend. It is a tireless enemy that can tear and eat at you. On the other hand, guilt is an extension of the human ego that in some circumstances can act as a moral barometer. If you have committed a terrible act, guilt is a consequence and can be an incentive not to repeat it. The lesson to be learned from guilt is to avoid the behaviors that caused you to feel it. Learn from your guilt.

Sometimes, though, inappropriate guilt weighs so heavily on us that we cannot forgive ourselves. Spirits know the importance of making amends and of forgiveness. They do not wish their loved ones in the material world to suffer from unresolved guilt issues.

In the cases of Doris, Ruth, and Buckey, spirits of their loved ones on the Other Side communicated to give them the chance to release themselves from self-flagellation by presenting the insights necessary to forgive events over which they had no control.

Reinhold Niebuhr wrote a familiar prayer, a version of which is most commonly associated with Alcoholics Anonymous. This prayer may also provide guidance to many suffering from guilt:

> *God, give us grace to accept with serenity the*
> *things that cannot be changed, the courage to*
> *change the things that should be changed, and the*
> *wisdom to distinguish the one from the other.*

A MESSAGE OF forgiveness from the Other Side is one of the many benefits of spirit contact. Feeling forgiven can be an important step toward acceptance of death, allowing inner peace to grow in place of guilt and remorse.

10

Forgiving Those
on the Other Side

*T*hese words are attributed to Saint Francis
of Assisi: "It is in pardoning that we are pardoned." It may take the virtue of a saint to truly
forgive someone who has harmed you, especially
in situations related to a death. The ability to forgive is complicated further when rape, incest, or
murder are involved. Forgiveness is the most complex of all the virtues. It is not easy, and it may
take years to fully forgive yourself or to forgive
someone else.

When the person who has harmed you is already dead, you may feel it is not possible to forgive that person, or you may find you are not ready or don't know how to do so. However, redemption is not the sole province of the material world. God gives us the opportunity to forgive those on the Other Side, even though it may be painful to do so.

Forgiveness is a present you give yourself, offering freedom from unhappy, hurtful memories. Until you free yourself from the past, you will always be its prisoner.

Christine, a strikingly beautiful woman in her forties, had a difficult time with forgiveness. One night I conducted a reading for her. Initially, her grandmother came through with some beautiful messages for Christine, but then another spirit made his presence known.

The spirit was a paternal grandfather. As I described his appearance, I felt something strange. This spirit emanated an almost smarmy sensation. I found this unusual, since family members normally do not present themselves in this way. Often family members show up with messages of love to say how happy they are. However, this spirit was asking Christine to forgive him.

The spirit told me what he had done to Christine when he was living in the material world. I realized the information was accurate from the expression of fear on Christine's face.

"Get him away from me! I'm not comfortable with him around! I don't ever want him around me!" Christine said. The terror in her eyes confirmed that her grandfather had sexually molested her when she was a child.

At the spirit's request, I relayed, "He is sorry and asks your forgiveness."

Christine replied, "I don't care what he wants, get him away from me."

I stopped the reading, and her grandfather's spirit receded. I felt compassion for Christine, thanked her for her time, and said no more about it.

A week later, I saw Christine at a social function, elegantly dressed, as usual. Always gracious, she asked gently, "Mark, would it be okay if we talked about the reading last week?"

"Of course," I said. We stepped out to a private spot.

She needed to talk. "I'm sorry for getting angry with you during the reading, but I think you know now that my grandfather molested me."

"I understand. I didn't mean to cause you any pain or bring back terrible memories," I apologized.

"It's not that, Mark. Because of what he did, I've undergone therapy for years to deal with it. In many ways, I've forgiven him—but I just can't let go of my anger. What he did to me was disgusting. I'm working on it, and I truly would like to forgive him. It's just so hard for me even to think about it, much less feel forgiveness."

"I can't even imagine what you have been through," I told her.

Christine continued, "I don't want him around me. It shook me up when he appeared. I wasn't ready for that."

"Thank you for letting me know this. I felt bad after the reading," I admitted.

Christine hugged me. "Mark, you're a medium. I'm sure things like this happen to you often. You were just doing your job."

I was grateful for her understanding.

Who could blame Christine for feeling the way she did? What her grandfather did was despicable. Although she had worked through the shock and trauma of being molested, she did not yet have the strength to forgive this man. She still felt hurt, disgust, anger, and violation at the thought of him.

However, before she left that evening, Christine offered a profound thought. "I'd like to share something I've learned. If you cannot forgive someone out of your love for that person, then you must forgive that person because of the love you have for yourself. If you still can't forgive that person, ask God to forgive him."

Clearly, Christine will be able to let go of the sorrow this man's acts and betrayal caused her. She has accepted what she cannot change and is on the path to inner peace.

When the Dalai Lama was asked how to forgive someone, he replied, "Tell the wrongdoer that you forgive him, and then turn around and run away as fast as you can."

Once you forgive someone, it doesn't mean you have given that person a license to continue to abuse you. And it doesn't mean the abuser isn't responsible for his or her actions.

When teaching how to forgive, my friend Father Sonny liked to quote Earnie Larson, who said, "Let go, let God." When you can let go of the sorrow triggered by the person who originally angered you, then you will be able to hold on to the love you have within you. If you still cannot find it in your heart to forgive someone, then, as Christine said, "Ask God to forgive him."

Even Jesus said, "Father, forgive them, for they know not what they do." He didn't say "*I* forgive them." (Although I have no doubt that Jesus *did* forgive them.)

The second part of that statement, "for they know not what they do," can have application for all of us. How many times does someone commit a crime or harmful act out of impulse or selfishness? These unthinking, self-centered behaviors have long-term repercussions.

Other times there may be no rational reasons why harmful acts were committed. It may just be a case of "they know not what they do."

ERIK CALLED ME and made an appointment for a reading, asking if he could bring two other family members with him. It is not unusual for more than one person to come for a reading. I believe that it can be beneficial to have moral support when engaging in spirit contact, which can often be extremely emotional.

Erik, his wife, Cindy, and his brother, Pete, all arrived at my office. I began the reading, and the spirit of Erik and Pete's father came through right away. He was obviously the person they wanted to contact. I got the distinct impression that he had not been on the Other Side very long.

"He died two months ago," Erik told me.

While this might have been a little soon for a reading, Erik and his family seemed as though they were ready for the contact. Their father presented them each with a message of hope and healing. Even though it had been only two months since their father's death, they definitely seemed prepared for this contact. What they didn't expect was the other spirit who decided to make an appearance.

"Your father is stepping aside so someone else can come through," I explained. "This spirit looks a lot like you, Erik. Actually, like an older version of you."

Suddenly, all three of them became very quiet. The two brothers shot each other concerned glances.

"This man is connected to you through your father's side of the family. I believe it is your father's brother."

"Sounds like him," Erik said. "This is interesting."

"He needs to ask you to forgive him," I described.

Normally, spirits on the Other Side appear happy and free of the burdens of this life. This one seemed troubled. He appeared to have unfinished business that he wanted to resolve. This spirit also presented a challenge because he was concealing something from me, and I couldn't discern what it was.

"What does he want?" Pete asked.

"Why does he want to talk to us?" Cindy interjected.

"He says he ruined a lot of Christmases," I conveyed.

"That's for sure," Erik replied.

"He keeps asking for forgiveness," I relayed. "He says, 'You have to forgive me. There is no one left who is willing to forgive me.'"

"Why is he asking for forgiveness now?" Erik asked.

"He wants you to know he was depressed. It was chemical. He says it made him angry and paranoid," I responded.

"No kidding," Erik commented.

"He felt everyone was watching him and talking about him," I explained.

"I don't know if we should listen to him," Pete said.

"No, let's hear what he has to say," Erik insisted.

"He says he is reflecting on the pain he's caused. 'Over here I'm fine, I can see it all so clearly now. Please forgive me. She does,'" I conveyed.

The three family members looked at each other, whispering among themselves. Finally Erik said, "Tell him we forgive him."

"He wants to thank you," I said, "and he wants to tell you 'every penny counts.'"

"That's our uncle," Erik explained. "He had a lot of financial problems."

"He is thanking you again—and now he's receded," I said.

"You're probably wondering what he needed forgiveness for," Pete said.

"It is not important that I understand the message, only that you do. I have to admit, I am curious, though," I said.

"That was our father's brother, our uncle Mike," Erik explained. "I look just like him, so when you told me he looked like an older version of me, I knew it was him."

"Okay, so what is he so sorry about?" I asked.

"He had a lot of problems with depression and needed to be on medication. One day, he snapped. He took a gun and murdered his wife, and then he turned the gun on himself. So, yeah, he ruined a lot of Christmases," Erik told me.

"That's horrible. I'm so sorry."

"That's only part of it," Pete said. "This was his second wife, and even though they didn't have any children, Uncle Mike had a daughter from his first marriage. She gave birth just two days after he had murdered his wife and committed suicide. This happened years ago, and our cousin has never been able to forgive her father. Having a baby is supposed to be a happy time, but it sure wasn't for her. I don't know if she would ever want to hear from him. Everyone in the family is still really angry, and I can't blame them."

"That might be why he said there's no one left willing to forgive him," I said. "You may be the only ones."

This was an extremely sensitive situation. The child of this spirit will suffer from this trauma for the rest of her life. Although his daughter may not have been receptive to contact with the spirit of her father, he did wish to seek forgiveness. From his new vantage point on the Other Side, he realized he was not in his right mind when this happened.

Obviously, when someone commits suicide, it inflicts tremendous suffering upon surviving loved ones. It is possible that the person committing suicide may have been emotionally unstable or so incoherent due to drug or alcohol abuse that he may not have fully grasped what he was doing.

There are situations where suicide is committed as a form of revenge or to intentionally inflict as much suffering as possible upon family and friends. For people with such motivations, it is easy for the survivors to be angry, resentful, remorseful, and confused. The survivors face a lifetime of wondering why. They also suffer from guilt and deep emotional pain. Although it is incredibly difficult to resolve forgiveness issues in these cases, we must strive to have compassion for those who commit suicide.

In a situation where someone has committed suicide to inflict pain upon you, this may become the great spiritual test of your life. If you can even in some small measure forgive that person and do your best to let go of the sorrow but hold on to the love, you will begin to accomplish an enormous spiritual life lesson. This is not easy, and it may take a lifetime to achieve this forgiveness, but doing so may be your task in this life.

Spirits who committed suicide in their human form may not get a free pass. Due to the tremendous suffering the suicide inflicts, the spirit is kept from ascending higher into the Light. Spiritually, the deceased may not be able to progress and as a result is connected more to the material world from which they intended to disconnect. Unfinished business with survivors must be resolved.

SOMETIMES WE ARE angry with someone just because they died. Our loved ones on the Other Side are constantly looking out for us and are aware of this. If only we can learn to listen, they can help us heal.

While studying with tutors from the Arthur Findlay College for the Advancement of Psychic Science, I was selected to participate in a mediumship demonstration. A medium is asked to stand before a group of people and connect with a spirit who has a message for someone in the audience. This audience consisted of about forty students who were mediums, as well as other psychically inclined individuals. As I stood before the group, I saw the spirits of several young males in their teens and early twenties; all were willing to make contact.

At first, I almost laughed as I was describing them, because they seemed like a rowdy bunch. None of them seemed bad; they were more like the mischievous types who often get sent to the principal's office.

What at first appeared as a light-hearted bunch of guys from the Other Side suddenly turned into a much heavier situation when I came to the stark realization that their parents were sitting before me in the audience. It became crystal clear that these bereaved parents had turned to the development of their psychic senses and the use of mediumship abilities as a means of coping with their loss and grief.

The overwhelming sensation of sadness experienced by these grieving parents hit me like a truck. These people were heartbroken and hurting. They missed their sons.

I saw that many of the young men had died in accidents, some by their own hand. One spirit came forth: a handsome, blond, clean-cut, collegiate-looking young man.

This was an intense clairvoyant experience, since he appeared so clearly that I could see him standing next to me. The spirits of the other young men stepped aside and receded from my perception. I knew this was the spirit who needed to make contact.

I described his physical appearance. "This young man had an upbeat personality and was intelligent and hardworking. He had been in college majoring in a technical field such as engineering or computer science."

I was drawn to a woman who was sitting in the front row.

"He wants to get a message through to his mother," I said as I looked at the woman.

The woman looked up and said, "He's my son."

Then I felt dizzy. My head was swimming. The room felt like it was going round and round. Something was not right in this young man's head before he died. I recognized this sensation as death from a drug overdose. "His death was sudden, unexpected, and unplanned," I explained.

Her tears confirmed all of this. Although I must always remain professional, it broke my heart to see this woman in so much grief.

The spirit sent his mother, Barbara, messages of love and closeness. Bouquets of flowers—mums, carnations, and roses—were projected. He showed me one of the symbols I associate with love: a huge red Valentine heart in the midst of all the flowers.

Barbara looked at me intently and said, "My son and I were very close. He died of an accidental drug overdose at a party in college."

As mediums, we must be compassionate without getting caught up between the emotions of the spirit and of the person for whom we are conducting the reading. I was doing my best in this situation, but it was difficult. The love between mother and son was overwhelming. Maybe the realization that the bond between parent and child cannot be broken, even by physical death, struck a chord in me.

I conveyed his messages. "He knows you miss him horribly. He knows how you brood for him, night after night. He feels your pain when you grieve for him, even when you're all alone and no one can hear you cry."

Barbara stared at me as tears ran down her cheeks.

"He wants you to know he is fine, and he loves you. He doesn't want you to suffer so much and be so crushed."

I was moved to hug Barbara and told her so. Slowly, she stood. I embraced Barbara as her son's words came out of my mouth: "I'm sorry, Mom. I didn't mean to do it."

Barbara sobbed in my arms. I sobbed with her, sensing this was a major turning point in her grief. Finally, she was ready to accept his passing and begin to forgive him.

When we learn to let go, we are not deleting that person from our life. Instead, we are making room to grow spiritually and emotionally and freeing our energy to do so. In the material world, there are physical and spiritual components to our relationships. However, in accepting the passing of a loved one, we must acknowledge that our relationship no longer possesses a physical component and is now purely spiritual. A purely spiritual relationship is on a much deeper level.

A spirit will come to us when the spirit needs to give a message to us or senses we need them in some way. Barbara's wonderful son knew his mother was suffering. He reached out to her at a time when she was ready to receive his message. It was still immensely difficult for her, but this brave woman came to accept the passing of her son and began working to forgive him.

HOLDING ON TO anger, resentment, and hatred is like drinking poison and expecting the other person to die. Think about that. Focus on someone who has angered you. Does the mere thought of that person irritate you? Just picturing that person may make your heart rate increase. Do you grind your teeth? Do you relive an encounter that was ugly and heated? How much distress are you feeling?

Now apply this to someone who is dead. The person against whom you hold the anger is already physically dead. So who is that person hurting now? Who is hurting you now? *You* are hurting you. The negative emotions of fear, anger, and resentment cause tremendous distress, which can manifest in emotional, spiritual, and physical ways.

Such emotional blocks can prevent you from experiencing the joy of love. You cannot truly be spiritual if the space within you is filled with negativity. Physically, negative emotions can make you sick. Think of the word *disease*. Its root word is *ease*. Dis-ease is a lack of ease within you. Forgiveness is one way to restore that ease.

Hatred is an extremely negative emotion. It stems from feelings of humiliation, embarrassment, and violation at the deepest core level. It is an emotionally injured person's flailing attempt to protest against these feelings. Unfortunately, hatred can become a way of life. It is affection for affliction, so to speak. As perverse as this may be, it rises to the level of pride in carrying the injury. Hatred provides a motivation to fight back, yet it often results in feeding the fires of rage. Rage may lead to revenge as the fires continue to burn, refueling again and again. It is healing to take whatever steps are necessary to end hatred. A first step might be to try to put the situation into a healthier perspective by removing yourself from the triggers that heat up the feelings. Forgiveness is one way to do this.

If harboring anger, resentment, and hatred is like drinking poison, then forgiveness is the antidote. The antidote may at first have an unpleasant taste, yet it can become the flavor that removes the bitterness from life.

IN JANUARY 2009, during the Space Coast Writers' Guild convention in Cocoa Beach, Florida, word spread that I was a medium who had written about spirit contact.

Over dinner I chatted with a few of the other writers. One of the writers at our table was a middle-aged woman with shoulder-length blond hair. I couldn't help but notice her soulful blue eyes as she said to me, "I heard you communicate with spirits. I communicate with my son."

"It's great that you can do that—" My words stopped abruptly when I saw her nametag: Vicki Rios-Martinez. I practice law in the county where the case of her son's murder had been tried. I knew the judge and the attorneys, both prosecution and defense. Vicki Rios-Martinez was the mother of Junny Rios-Martinez Jr., an eleven-year-old boy who was kidnapped, forcibly raped, and then brutally murdered on April 18, 1991. The killer, Mark Dean Schwab, was only one month out of prison for the rape of another young boy when he kidnapped and murdered Junny.

I tried to cover my faux pas. "I'm so sorry, Mrs. Rios-Martinez. I hope you didn't think I was being flippant. I meant no offense. It's just—I'm always elated to meet other people with mediumistic ability."

"I understand," she smiled sweetly. "And please call me Vicki. I'd like to talk with you tomorrow, if that's okay?"

"Of course," I said.

The next day, around noon, we were on a lunch break. I saw Vicki in the hotel lobby. "Would you consider conducting a reading for me?" she asked.

"It would be an honor," I replied. I looked around the crowded hotel lobby and spotted a door to the pool cabana. The two of us slipped outside. We could hear the pounding of the surf nearby. Finding a quiet spot near the pool, we stood under the shade of palm trees. When we were comfortable, I said two prayers and began the reading.

Initially, an older woman came through. I described her appearance to Vicki.

"That is my stepmother. Junny loved her; they were very close."

"She's not alone. There's someone with her who's now coming through. He's a whimsical, playful presence, someone who was very active during life," I said. "I see a boy running on the beach, chasing seagulls, lots of seagulls. I also see an image of the ocean where the water is smooth and glassy but the waves are big, ideal for surfing."

"Junny was a surfer, and the large, glassy waves were his favorite," Vicki said with a slight smile.

"Excuse me, do you know where the restaurant is?" a woman asked, interrupting us.

"*No!*" Vicki and I replied in unison. Clearly we needed privacy to continue.

The woman took a few steps back before turning toward the hotel door.

"Mark," Vicki said, "it's such a beautiful day. Why don't we continue this at the beach?"

"Good idea," I said as we left poolside. We walked the short distance from the hotel to the beach. It was a warm, sunny day, and the crisp ocean air smelled clean and fresh. On the boardwalk along the beach, we stopped to take in the view. Just yards away on the sand, a flock of more than 100 seagulls were sunning themselves and preening their feathers. We looked out past the beach to the deep blue water of the Atlantic Ocean. Numerous surfers were riding the large, glassy waves. In view of the water, the glassy waves, and the seagulls on the beach, we both came to the same conclusion.

"If this isn't a sign from Junny, I don't know what is," Vicki said.

"Junny is definitely here. I see him. But I must admit, I recognize his image from the news. However, at this moment, I'm seeing him on a basketball court," I explained.

"That's odd. Junny didn't play basketball," Vicki said.

"Well, I keep seeing that image over and over. It seems important," I told her.

"Wait, I know what it is!" Vicki put her hand to her mouth. "There's a basketball court in a park that was named in honor of Junny."

"He is showing me a kite—he's holding a kite, and he is saying, 'I don't want you to feel bad about the kite. It's not your fault,'" I conveyed.

Vicki looked intently at me. "A month before he was murdered, he won a kite-making contest. The newspaper printed his picture. Junny was a good-looking boy, and that photo is what attracted Mark Schwab to my son. I've always felt somehow responsible for allowing the photo to be in the newspaper."

Although it was a sunny day, I shivered and felt goose-bumps. Abruptly, I began to feel incredibly angry. I clenched my fists, and my fingernails dug into my palms. "Junny is showing me the image of a man who is angry and hurt. He's medium height, with a dark complexion. Wears a mustache. I feel I want to scream out loud how angry I am! He is connected to Junny but is not on the Other Side. He's still here!"

"You're describing my husband, Junny's father," Vicki explained.

"Well, Junny also feels his father's pain, and he wants—even needs—his dad to let go of it. This bond of pain and his father's anguish anchors Junny here," I conveyed. "Junny wants the family to let go of the grieving. He says he has other things he needs to do."

"Junny told me the same thing when he communicated from the Other Side," Vicki said thoughtfully. "He has a job to do, but first we need to let go."

I replied, "Your son has the best vibration; he's definitely in the Light. This young man had a lot of love."

"Yes. Junny was such a happy boy, and we miss him so," she said wistfully.

"There's a memento, a small box. It is a secret. You keep it in the kitchen, near the refrigerator. It has something to do with his ashes," I explained.

"I keep his ashes in a container above the refrigerator in the kitchen. No one knows about that," Vicki confided softly.

"Wait, now there is another presence coming through. Good lord!" I put my hands over my mouth.

"Who is it?" Vicki asked.

"I feel despicable. This spirit feels like an echo, as if it is hollow. It's like the reflection of a person, not a complete person. It's an odd sensation that I'm feeling anger not from a spirit, but *at* a spirit. It's him. It's Schwab." My hand pushed down my other arm like I was trying to remove slime.

Vicki looked solemn but stood straight. "Go on."

"Are you sure? I can ask him to leave," I said.

"No, I want to hear what he has to say," Vicki said softly. "I didn't get to say something to him before he was executed."

"Schwab's spirit feels distant, almost cold. He's on the Other Side but not in the Light. He's definitely not up at the same frequency Junny is on."

She nodded her head.

"I feel pains in my head. He's indicating he had a lot of headaches and that his mind was like a TV screen filled with static." I paused. "I can only interpret this to mean that he was not right in his head. His mind was disturbed, confused, and governed by impulse."

"What else?" she asked.

"I can see an image of an empty but filthy garbage can. That's how he sees himself: like an empty garbage can, filthy and empty," I repeated. "He has a message for you."

"Tell me whatever he wants to say," Vicki prodded.

"He's asking forgiveness. He is sorry for all the pain he caused you, Junny, and so many people," I relayed. "I also get the impression that Junny isn't the only person he's murdered."

Vicki raised her eyebrows, and her eyes widened. "There was evidence, hair and blood evidence, at the scene that didn't match Junny or Mark Schwab," she confided. "I don't think law enforcement did any follow-up on it."

I took a deep breath before resuming. "I feel a strong wave of disgusting emotion. Animalistic sexual urges ran through him when he was alive. It's sickening."

Vicki stood her ground, her eyes locked on mine.

"He's really making me angry, Vicki. I apologize. I'm supposed to be objective, but this spirit fills me with revulsion," I said through clenched teeth. "He's sorry, he knows what he's done. He begs forgiveness and is reflecting on everything he put you and your family through."

Once I said that, the energy changed. The waves of anger and revulsion that had flooded me suddenly ceased and were replaced by feelings of intense serenity and love. An extremely positive spirit had come to my rescue. "It's Junny now," I said, feeling tears rolling down my cheeks. "I can hardly believe what he is saying. Junny says, 'We must forgive him. Over here he isn't bad.'"

Vicki spoke up. "I do forgive Schwab."

I was flabbergasted. "Really?"

"I felt cheated at his execution—July 1, 2008." Junny's mother looked out over the ocean, then continued. "By the time my family was allowed to witness Schwab's execution, he was already sedated in preparation for the lethal injection.

That wasn't how I'd planned it. I worked hard over many years to resolve my grief and anguish and come to some resolution about Junny's horrible death and the loss of our son. Before the execution, there was something I needed Schwab to know. I needed to look into his eyes. I needed him to look deeply into my eyes and for him to find the forgiveness there. I wanted to show him forgiveness through my eyes in a way that he could feel it before he died. I wish I could have said directly to him, face to face, that I forgave him."

We sat silently for a few moments, both of us wiping the tears from our eyes. "You just did," I said as I felt the unsettled spirit of Schwab recede. "He knows now."

"I'm glad I'm telling the psychic lawyer this," Vicki said softly. "After Junny was murdered, my husband and I, and all our family, worked to change the laws relating to sex offenders. We started with the Junny Rios-Martinez Act, which takes gain time away from sex offenders so they don't get out of prison early. Working with politicians has been frustrating. They're more concerned with building bridges than with protecting children. I guess children don't vote or pay taxes, so very little is changed for their benefit. Being in jail doesn't cure a sex offender, and treatment doesn't work. Something needs to change," she said. "We've been speaking publicly about the legal system, victims, and their rights—and the enduring loss of a child. I've written a book about it, *The ABCs of Grief*. My book is a journey through grief letter by letter, emotion by emotion, from the valley of the shadow of death to the light at the end of the tunnel. It takes one from anger to ascension by suggesting ways to survive grief—even thrive in spite of it. That's why I came to this conference. I don't want other children to be hurt and die the way Junny did. But to do this work, I had to be able to forgive Schwab. I couldn't carry that rage and hurt and be able to speak about forgiveness."

Schwab's spirit was on the Other Side but not in a place that I would call the Light. It seemed he was in a hollow and distant place devoid of the Light in order to reflect on the horrors he had inflicted on so many people. Perhaps he must work to emerge from that pit of emptiness and will eventually ascend into the Light. Only God has the power to make that decision.

I've never met anyone quite like Vicki Rios-Martinez. I struggled to grasp how she could forgive the man who murdered her little boy. Her inner strength and her deep faith in God and in the powers of redemption and forgiveness were awe inspiring.

I had always wondered what it would be like to meet a saint, and on that beautiful, sunny winter day before the sparkling sea, I think I did.

11

Gratitude and Consolation
from the Other Side

*T*here is an old saying: "No good deed goes unpunished." I suppose this bit of sarcasm means when you extend a kindness that somehow isn't appreciated, it ends up being a burden of some sort. It may be true that doing the right thing can often be difficult and may require effort and self-sacrifice. From a spiritual standpoint, it is better to look at doing something positive for another person with *this* saying in mind: "No good deed goes unnoticed."

Not all messages from the Other Side are about forgiveness or the resolution of wrongs. Many times, spirits are happy just to communicate with someone here in the material world. At times, spirits want to acknowledge a kindness; this often involves telling a loved one "thank you." These messages of gratitude are not only comforting, they are extremely healing.

The healing comes from knowing that your loved one in spirit is happy, safe, and free of the ills that plagued him or her while living in the material world. It is also important for a person here to know that the sacrifices he or she made for someone who died were appreciated.

Death and dying are the most serious and emotionally gripping events anyone has to face. Not all deaths are sudden and unexpected. All too often, the death of a loved one is a protracted process. It is agonizing to watch someone you love die slowly of an incurable disease.

Caring for a dying person is a tremendous responsibility. When a terminally ill person comes close to death, there may be support for that person from family, friends, or organizations such as hospice. Fear may be eased for the dying person if he or she does not have to face death alone. For the loved ones of the dying person, it is consoling to have a support system assist them in coping with the death and its aftermath.

Perhaps the most famous caregiver of all time was Mother Teresa. Mother Teresa was a Catholic nun who, while living in Calcutta, India, created an order known as the Sisters of Charity. These nuns dedicate their lives to helping those for whom no one else cares. Mother Teresa believed that no one should die feeling that his or her life had no meaning. She set a perfect example of the perfect caregiver.

Sadly, in many instances, caregivers do not have a support system to assist them in caring for someone who is incapacitated and/or terminally ill. The caregiver must face this overwhelming responsibility alone. Caring for a dying person is physically demanding, emotionally draining, expensive, and time-consuming. It is a responsibility that can take years. Caregiving may also seem to be a thankless task. That is why it may be healing for caregivers to know that their efforts were recognized and greatly appreciated.

Based on messages received in many of the readings I've conducted, spirits are grateful to people here in the material world who cared for them when they were ill and who helped them transition to the Other Side. This was the case with Jane, a woman I met while visiting the Arthur Findlay College for the Advancement of Psychic Science in England. Jane was from Scotland. It would be hard not to like her, as she was one of those warm, sensitive, and compassionate people who emit the inner light of goodness.

During the reading, the spirit of what appeared to be an older man came through. "This gentleman has a receding hair line. He is a strong and manly man who loved his little girl very much," I explained.

"Sounds like me dad," Jane replied.

"I see him in a hospital bed. I don't believe, though, that he died in a hospital. It seems as if he died at home. He acknowledges that you were constantly by his side. He is lying on very white linen. He insisted on white linen—does that make sense?" I asked.

"Aye, that it does," Jane replied.

"Ouch," I said, as I felt a slight stabbing sensation in my arm.

"Are you okay, then?" Jane asked with concern.

"I'm fine," I replied. "He was just letting me know that he had an intravenous tube in his left arm. He didn't like that too much. His death was not unexpected. It took quite a while for him to pass from cancer."

Jane acknowledged this by nodding solemnly. Her eyes were like pools of deep blue water.

"He says, 'You took care of me. So much fell on you, and you had to do it alone. You picked up the pieces and pulled the whole family together. I want to thank you for being there.'"

"Thank you, Dad, and thank you for bringing him through, Mark," Jane said.

"And he says you did a great job at his funeral," I conveyed. "Good eulogy. He enjoyed it."

HOLLY AND RON have been happily married for years. Both are professionals in the mental health field. Despite their happy appearance, they have suffered immensely. I met Holly at a support group for parents of deceased children. Her adult son, Glenn, had recently died of colon cancer. This brave young man had fought this insidious disease for two years before he passed. Both of them came to me for a reading with the hope of contact with Glenn.

"He says when he was a kid, he liked to skateboard and ride a bicycle a lot," I conveyed. "He really had a joy for life. On the surface, he appeared carefree. Yet beyond the façade, he was a serious person. I would describe his personality as deep and intense."

"That's what he was like," Holly acknowledged.

"He wants you to know how much he enjoyed the close bond he had with you." Although I felt this would be something Ron would have done with him, I felt as if the message were intended for Holly, so I looked to her as I said, "You took him fishing and hunting. You did a lot of outdoor activities together."

"I *was* the one who took him hunting and fishing," Holly confirmed. "I always enjoyed being outdoors with my son."

"He is now showing me many images of several different things the two of you did together. One memory in particular is being presented. He says it is significant. The two of you were planting flowers when you noticed a butterfly on a fern. You sat on the ground together to watch," I explained.

"I do remember that. It was such a beautiful day," Holly said.

"He's saying that this day shaped all the days that came after. Glenn also says that there was an issue between you that you worked through that day. This made both of you very happy. He's not giving me specifics—he says you'll know what he means," I conveyed. It was clear that this had been a private moment between mother and son. As much as I wanted to ask about its significance, I realize that if a spirit wants me to know something, the spirit will let me know. Otherwise, my job is just to present the messages as accurately as possible.

"I understand exactly what he means and why it was significant. Thank you, Glenn," Holly said, maintaining her composure although her eyes were beginning to water.

Glenn's spirit now directed my attention to Ron. "Now he has a message for you, Ron," I said. "Glenn wants to thank you for spending time with him. He really wants you to know how grateful he is that you were a part of his life," I relayed.

Ron looked very intent. It seemed that, like Holly, he was working to maintain his composure. A single tear ran down his face. "Glenn was my stepson. We were always cordial to each other, but it never seemed to me that we were that close. I guess I always wanted him to think of me as his father. It means a lot to me to know he appreciated me," Ron explained.

"Glenn is showing me a little girl who is here, meaning she is not on the Other Side. This girl appears to be his daughter. She is riding a pink bicycle. He is concerned because he was not there to teach her how to ride the bike. Although he was alive at the time, he was too ill to be able to spend time with her," I told them. "He wishes he could be there for her."

"That is our granddaughter," Holly said.

"Let Glenn know I'll be there to help her," Ron added.

"This next message is for a woman. She is a brunette with very white skin. She is not handling his death well and is full of anxiety. This seems to be his wife."

"That is Glenn's wife," Holly confirmed. "She is having a very difficult time with his death."

"He loved her so much—still does and always will. He wants her to know that. He also wants to thank her for helping him through his illness," I explained.

Glenn stepped aside as Holly's paternal grandmother came through. "This is a physically small woman with a round face. She was very strong emotionally and physically. I see her holding a bunch of grapes and crushing them with her hand. The grape juice is running down her arm," I told them, describing the imagery.

Holly and Ron looked as perplexed as I felt. "What does that mean?" Holly asked.

I closed my eyes and asked for the grandmother's spirit to explain the message. After a few moments, I conveyed her answer. "She is telling me the crushing of the grapes means that sometimes life gets tough. The juice running down her arm means that sometimes things look bad, like life is a waste. But with strength and perseverance, an event can turn into something beautiful, just as crushed grapes can become something sweet."

"She always had an interesting way of explaining things," Holly commented.

"She says your strength comes from her, and you've done a good job. She is proud of you," I told Holly.

Holly smiled. "She was a strong woman. I'm glad she feels that way about me."

Glenn's spirit returned for a final message. "I see Glenn in a barn, petting a dark brown horse with a white nose," I said.

"That was Glenn's horse! He loved that horse!" Holly said elatedly.

"Glenn is taking the horse for a ride through a golden field of wheat toward green hills, into the yellow sunset. These colors come with a meaning. Gold is a spiritual color, green is a healing color, and the yellow sunset is happiness. He means now he is happy, he is at peace, and he is free of the pain," I explained.

"Sounds like he's in Heaven," Holly said.

"It does indeed," I replied.

THERE ARE TIMES when spirits want to acknowledge a kindness or offer a message of consolation. The reading I conducted for Marilyn was a great example of how you can be surprised by some of the spirits who make an appearance. When I met Marilyn, she told me, "I have a lot of dead people I'd like to talk to. I'm seventy, and so many of my friends and relatives have died."

"The first individual coming through is actually a little dog, a Scottish terrier. He's transmitting feelings of pure love," I said.

"That was my dog. My mother gave him to me when I was about twelve years old. I loved that little dog," Marilyn said, smiling.

"Now there is a young man coming forward. He's a teenager, very shy," I explained.

"I'm not sure who that is," Marilyn said.

"He was killed by a sudden impact; it feels like a car crash. You were in high school together," I conveyed.

"Oh, now I know who that is. He was such a nice boy. This was over fifty years ago. Why is he contacting me?" Marilyn asked.

"He says he always had a crush on you, but he was too shy to do anything about it. Just knowing you always made him feel happy. He wants to thank you for that."

"That is so sweet. I liked him, too. Back then, I was too shy to take the first step," Marilyn said. "I wonder what would've happened if I had."

SOMETIMES, THE MANNER in which spirits present their messages may not always be warm and loving. When a person dies, his or her personality remains intact. A person's memories and his or her likes and dislikes continue on in spirit. I've found that a spirit will communicate in much the same manner he or she did when alive. If someone was kind and polite in physical life, the spirit will be kind and polite. If the person was funny and humorous, the spirit will be funny and humorous. And if the person was rude and abrupt, that, too, is how the spirit may be.

During a reading for Stephanie, two spirits wanted to extend gratitude and consolation; they just went about it in different ways. Her father was the first to come through. "The energetic vibration of this spirit is dense and strong. The best way I can explain his vibration is like the low E string on a bass guitar," I explained.

"Dad was really intense," Stephanie said.

"He is very abrupt. His communication is short and clipped, almost forceful," I described.

Stephanie rolled her eyes. "That's how he was. My dad was extremely quick and rude with people, especially his family."

"He says he loves his family, but he shouldn't have to tell you that," I relayed.

Stephanie gave a slight smile.

"He also wants to say something about the last words he said to you—he didn't mean them," I conveyed.

Stephanie looked at me for a few moments before she spoke. "He was terminally ill. His condition became critical, and hospice called to inform us. I was the first one to get there. My mother and sister were on their way. The last thing he said to me before he slipped into a coma was, 'You're my least favorite, but at least you're here.'"

I could see that those words had weighed heavily on her.

"Spirits communicate very much like they did when they were here," I explained. "Your father is no exception. He is very abrupt. He isn't exactly apologizing, but he knows what he said was wrong. He says 'I'm better now' and wants to emphasize how much he does love you."

"My father was a paranoid schizophrenic," Stephanie explained. "He could be very rude. Sometimes he said terrible things to us. It was like walking on eggshells when he was around. If he did something mean, which was most of the time, he usually made up for it later by doing something nice, but he never, ever apologized. That's what he's doing now. Even though he was difficult, I do love him, too."

"Your father is stepping aside so another spirit can come through. I'm having a hard time distinguishing if this spirit is male or female," I indicated.

"I don't understand," Stephanie said.

"I believe this is a male, and he has a strong feminine edge to him. He indicates his death was caused by blunt trauma, a sudden impact. It was unexpected. He has long hair. He is placing a lot of emphasis on his hair."

"Really?" Stephanie exclaimed. "That's Charlie. He was my cousin. He really did have great hair. In fact, it was beautiful. He was so good-looking. It's funny that you sensed a male-female thing. Everyone in the family always wondered if he was gay."

"That is interesting," I commented. "It seems as though he, too, may have still been wondering about that when he was alive. Usually, if the spirit believes it is relevant to the communication, the spirit will let me know what his or her sexual orientation in life was."

"Wouldn't surprise me a bit if he is still on the fence," Stephanie added.

"He has a great sense of humor. He keeps making me want to break out laughing, saying he doesn't kiss and tell," I conveyed.

"Charlie was hysterically funny," Stephanie said, smiling.

"Now he is getting a bit more serious. He wants you to understand that everything is fine, and you shouldn't feel bad or blame yourself. It wasn't your fault," I told her.

Stephanie stopped smiling, and her demeanor became more solemn. "He loved race cars, so one year for his birthday, I gave him Daytona Firecracker 400 tickets," Stephanie said. "On the way home from the race, he and a friend were killed in a car accident. I always wondered if they'd still be alive if I hadn't given him those tickets."

"He is showing me a field of green grass. He is holding a small flower. It is one of those wild daisies that grow here in Florida. It is a simple white flower with a yellow center and white petals. He says, 'Thank you for remembering me.'"

"I'm glad he knows about the flowers," Stephanie said softly as the tears flowed from her eyes. "He was always so thoughtful."

"I take this to mean that you understand the significance of the flower?" I asked.

"That's his grave. Every year on the anniversary of his death I go there. I pick a handful of those little white daisies and place them on his grave."

"He wants to let you know everything is fine. You shouldn't feel bad or blame yourself. He says he is never alone and is surrounded by a lot of family members. They're all together—he is projecting an image of a lot of people with him. They are having a picnic. It looks like they're eating fried chicken."

"We have a big family, but we weren't much for picnics and fried chicken, so I'm not sure that makes sense," Stephanie commented. "Why is he showing that imagery?"

"This is a strange response," I said. "He says 'We're like the dead Waltons.' He knows you'll understand, and he is laughing as he is saying that."

"Goodness," Stephanie said, wiping the tears from her eyes as she started to chuckle. "That is so funny. Remember that TV show back in the '70s, *The Waltons*?"

"Actually, I do," I replied.

"Remember how they were this really wholesome country family? They always got along and weren't that dysfunctional?" she recalled.

"I remember the show," I said, eager to understand the significance of the message.

"Well, Charlie and I always watched that show together, and he would joke, 'No one is crazy in that family. Why can't our family be like that?'"

It is easy to go through life thinking you haven't made a difference and that your life has had no meaning, yet it is not always apparent what a life is about. Meaning depends upon each person's experience and how that person influences and interacts with others. Some people are here to spread goodness and, unfortunately, others choose not to. Nevertheless, each life means something. Every life counts, every life matters, and we are all connected.

Even with that knowledge, it is easy to question the meaning of your own existence. It is true that not everyone can be rich and famous. Not everyone possesses awe-inspiring talents. Some of us seem to be just cogs in the wheels of the machine of society. Does this make your life lessons and experience here in the material world any less significant? The answer is no. This plane of existence is not the highest level of development we will experience. However, what we endure here and the acts we commit for good or for ill are part of the overall journey of our souls.

WHILE VISITING ENGLAND, I had the honor of conducting readings for several people. Amanda was one of them. "There's a grandfather coming through, and he looks like ..."

"Go on, it's quite all right," Amanda said.

"Remember those old Laurel and Hardy movies from back in the 1930s?" I asked.

"I do, indeed," Amanda said with a wry smile.

"He looks like Oliver Hardy. He's portly, wears a derby hat, and carries an umbrella. He likes to laugh, and when he does, he has a deep belly laugh." Amanda smiled at my description.

"That's my granddad, my mum's father," Amanda said cheerfully.

"When he was alive, he had swelling in his hands and feet. It feels like he had pretty bad cardiovascular disease, which he kept to himself. He was walking home from work one day, collapsed, and died soon after," I told her.

Amanda's eyes started to fill with tears.

"I'm sorry. When a spirit transmits this information to me, it isn't meant to be upsetting. This is part of the evidence a spirit conveys to identify who he or she was," I explained.

"No apologies necessary. I quite understand. Please, do go on," Amanda said, regaining her very English composure.

"He says he died in the 1950s, after the war and before the Beatles," I conveyed, thinking how interesting this spirit was at using these historical references. "He says that the happiest times of his life were watching his whole family sitting around the radio. It is one of those antique-looking radios, shaped like a gothic arch with big knobs," I described.

"That was our radio. I remember those nights well," Amanda said. "I was just a little girl."

"Here's the message he has for you: 'You were an oasis in my life. When I held you in my arms, you made me feel like the richest man in the world.'"

Amanda gazed at me thoughtfully.

"He wants to leave you with the image of a bright yellow flower—a buttercup," I conveyed.

The expression of joy and sadness in Amanda's eyes was something I will never forget.

"Whenever I see buttercups, I think of Granddad," she said softly. "They make me sad because I miss him so, but they make me happy too. He always said I was his little buttercup."

I ALSO CONDUCTED a reading in England for Sharon. It seemed to me that I was getting a lot of spirits who reminded me of old movie stars that day. Sharon's granny resembled film icon Bette Davis.

"Everyone always commented how she had those Bette Davis eyes," Sharon confirmed.

"She lived to be about ninety years old and had a lot of arthritis pain in her feet and hands, especially her left hand," I explained.

"Poor Granny, she suffered so," Sharon said.

"I'm seeing Peeps; I don't know if you have them in England. They're those marshmallow candies that look like little yellow chicks," I described.

"We absolutely have those in England. When I was very young, Granny always had a jar of them for us," Sharon acknowledged.

"Her message for you is one of gratitude. She says, 'You always wrote me thoughtful notes. You never made me feel alone. You always took time for me. Thank you. And remember—teach this to those around you,'" I conveyed.

After the reading, Sharon explained to me that when her granny got older, few family members visited her. Sharon felt bad about her granny being alone, so she always made the time to send her a little note, ring her up on the telephone, or just drop by for a visit. "It really wasn't much of a bother. I rather liked doing it," Sharon told me.

How many times, after an elderly relative has died, do you wish you had picked up the phone and called to say hello?

What may have seemed like a little effort on Sharon's part meant the entire world to her grandmother. It is easy to neglect people, especially the elderly, without realizing we are doing so. We get so caught up in our daily lives that we forget those who came before us while they are still alive. Sharon realized how important it was to take a little time out of her busy life to extend a thoughtful hand to someone who didn't get phone calls, visits from friends or family, or anything in the mail other than bills.

Think how it must feel to be forgotten—how lonely life would be. In life, many people feel insignificant—that they do not matter. Part of the message for Sharon was to teach others to make an effort to spend time with the elderly and those who are lonely. It isn't hard to do.

LYDIA CLAR IS an extraordinarily gifted psychic and medium. She was gracious enough to ask my friend Nancy and me to assist her when she was teaching a psychic development class. As part of an exercise during the class, I was asked to connect with and describe a spirit without acknowledging the recipient until I was finished.

"There is an older woman coming through who feels like a mother. Hearth, health, and home are extremely important to her. She spent a lot of time in deep contemplation and was a nurturing, caring, and compassionate woman. She took care of many people but often felt put upon and unappreciated. Her tears were quiet tears; she kept them to herself. She always wore a brave face. The person this message is directed to understood her; no one else did. She wants to thank you for realizing her life really did matter."

"Stop!" Beth, one of the students, called out. "You're making me cry."

Lydia Clar smiled gently and gestured for me to let Beth continue.

"That was my mother," Beth said, sobbing. "She felt that home and family were the most important things in life. She had a fireplace, a hearth she would sit beside while she read. She was the one who took care of all of her family members. One after the other, they became ill and died. She was the caregiver. My mother smiled on the outside, but on the inside, she was so sad. Everyone depended on her, but no one noticed how they were taking advantage of her. No one ever made time for her. I tried to, and I always hoped she realized I understood the pressure she was under and that she really was appreciated."

It is reassuring to know that an act of kindness, no matter how small we think it might be, is remembered by our loved ones on the Other Side. Most people are aware of the proverbial pebble—the one that falls into a pond with seemingly little impact after the initial splash. However, as the concentric rings in the water emanate outward from the splash, they touch many other things. Perhaps the influence is subtle, perhaps it is profound. By analogy, each person is the center of his or her own universe—or at least the universe as that person perceives it. One universe touches other universes like the concentric rings from a splash of a pebble in a pond.

This is why we must strive to keep our impact upon others positive. Positive actions will give rise to more positive actions, increasing concentric rings of goodness. Everything we do in life has repercussions, here in the material world and on the Other Side. Everyone matters, every life counts, and everything we do resounds in eternity.

12

Acceptance and
Inner Peace

he acceptance of death and the finding of inner
peace are some of the great lessons of Bud-
dhism. Although there are variations on the following tale, the message is universal.

A woman whose infant had just died heard of
a great teacher and miracle worker referred to
as the Buddha. Carrying the body of her baby,
she approached the Buddha. He was surrounded
by a large number of his followers and students.

The crowd parted, allowing the grief-stricken woman to come forward.

"Please," she implored. "Restore life to my baby."

The Buddha saw her pain and agony. He stood in front of her and looked upon her and upon the body of her little boy. With great compassion in his eyes, he said, "Before I do anything, you must first do something for me."

Feeling a glimmer of hope, she cried out, "I will do anything for you if you can bring my child back to life."

"Go to that village," the Buddha said, pointing to a town in the distance, "and bring me a handful of mustard seeds. But please, make sure they come only from a family who has not known death."

"Oh, thank you! I will," she said as she hurried off to the village, still clutching the body of her son.

Three days later, she returned.

"Did you bring me the handful of mustard seeds?" the Buddha asked.

"No, I went from door to door. Everyone understood my pain, but I couldn't find a family who hadn't known death. I even traveled to other villages, and it was the same. Every family has endured a death," she replied.

"What will you do now?" the Buddha asked.

"I am ready to bury my son," she replied.

"What did your journey teach you?" The Buddha looked upon her with love.

"That death is part of life and something everyone must accept," she replied.

The Buddha did not tell the woman to be happy and get over the death of her child. His teaching focused instead upon the acceptance of the reality of death.

We must realize that we can survive the shock and trauma that initially accompanies death. However, healing from the grief can take years, possibly an entire lifetime. Acceptance of a death doesn't mean you will stop missing your loved one. Rather, acceptance is part of the responsibility placed on us. Acceptance cannot be done for you; it is your undertaking. Over time, it won't hurt as much or as often. Through acceptance, you will gain wisdom and a new perspective. Acceptance is a painful lesson we must learn in order to evolve spiritually.

SOMETIMES WE NEED the guidance of spirit to accomplish this.

I was invited to an annual Christmas party hosted by my lifelong friends Mitch and Joan. They have a beautiful Old Florida–style home overlooking Crane Creek in a bucolic setting right out of a Highwayman painting: tall cypress trees, majestic oak trees, and sable palms tower over the dark brackish water ringed by cattails, lily pads, and hyacinths. The still waters of Crane Creek often form a perfect mirror image reflecting the world above.

Earlier in the book, I wrote about Joan. She, too, possesses mediumistic ability, which occurs primarily when she is sleeping. Over the years, she has delivered positive messages to several people who have loved ones on the Other Side.

At the Christmas party, Joan wanted to know about my work as a medium. We talked for a long time about spirit contact, and after a few hours, I needed to say good night. I wanted to leave but couldn't seem to do so. No matter what I tried, I couldn't make it through the crowd of partygoers to the front door. People kept talking, asking me questions.

Then a heavyset woman named Faye walked over and asked to talk to me. Faye was a kind woman who seemed depressed despite her smile. Joan agreed it would be a good idea if I spoke to Faye. I felt a strong spiritual presence around Faye. It became clear that she was the reason I couldn't leave the party. This spirit wanted me to communicate a message to Faye.

When Faye heard I was a medium, she wanted to receive a reading. At first, I wasn't sure this party was the ideal venue for a reading. However, it was a beautiful Florida winter evening, and the cloudless sky was filled with stars. We found a quiet spot behind our hosts' house on the dock overlooking Crane Creek, where we would not be interrupted. The still water of Crane Creek was smooth as glass. The mirror image of the stars reflecting in the water was spectacular.

Faye's mother's spirit came through. I conveyed a visual description of her: "She's an elderly woman in a wheelchair who seems like she had a long, slow decline before passing. In her lap, there's..."

"What's in Momma's lap?" Faye wanted to know.

"It is a . . ." I stalled for time.

"What is it? What do you see? Tell me!" Faye wasn't about to let up.

It's my job as a medium to accurately describe what I'm receiving, even if the image may have negative stereotypes associated with it.

"A black cat," I said reluctantly.

"A black cat! Oh my lord!" Faye exclaimed.

"Yes, but it's a small black cat," I said nervously, suddenly wishing I could be somewhere else.

"It *is* Momma! That's her cat Smokey!" Faye's face expressed elation. "She loved that little cat so much. He was her constant companion, and she took him everywhere with her."

With much relief, I explained the next message from the spirit. "Faye, your mother wants you to let go. You are anchoring her here."

"I can't do it. I can't. I'm so alone since Momma died," Faye admitted in her deep Southern drawl.

"Your mother needs you to let go so she can ascend higher into the Light. She asks you to accept her passing so you can heal," I conveyed.

"Heal? In what way?" Faye asked.

"You are harming yourself physically, and your mother is concerned about your health," I told her.

Then a spirit I assumed to be Faye's father came through. He was wearing a white T-shirt, horn-rimmed glasses, and blue jeans. His hair was parted on the side and slicked back with what looked like hair grease in a distinctly 1950s hair-style.

Faye laughed. "That's Daddy, all right. He always used hair grease. Daddy was a big Elvis fan, you know. He loved wear-ing T-shirts so much that we even decided to bury him in one."

Her father's spirit had a relaxed, easygoing personality. He had been on the Other Side much longer than Faye's mother. Interestingly, it felt as though he was not tethered to this world by Faye. It seemed she had let him go, and he had ascended. Her father's message, though, was insistent. "He wants you to know he is around you and it is important for you to move forward with your life. He asks you to let go of Momma so she can ascend higher into the Light."

Faye explained, "It was hard when Daddy passed. I learned to accept his death years ago. But I just couldn't bear it when Momma died. I feel guilty about her dying. Maybe I could've done something to change things."

"She knows you feel that way and wants you to under-stand you did everything you could. It was her time. Because of your pain and sadness, she won't leave you," I said.

"I know," Faye said. "I swear I feel her around me. So you're saying that isn't good for her?"

"Faye, I would like to share with you a message from my own mother. She said to me from the Other Side, 'Let go of the sorrow, but hold on to the love.' I feel this message may apply to you as well."

"Momma had cancer. I know there wasn't anything I could've done to save her, yet somehow I feel responsible," Faye told me.

"What she is saying," I explained, "is that your guilt and grieving anchors her to you. Love is such a powerful force that it transcends even physical death. Because you can't let go, she won't let go either as long as she knows you are suffering. This sorrow of guilt and unresolved grief is hurting you and anchoring her here. By letting go of that sorrow and remembering the love you had for her—and celebrating the love you still have for her—you may begin to heal."

"I know I have to accept Momma's passing and stop blaming myself," Faye admitted. "I know that...I guess I just needed something like this to help me."

I nodded in agreement as Faye interjected, "Guess Momma and Daddy want me to go on a diet, huh?"

Faye was nearly 100 pounds overweight as a result of overeating to numb her hurt. Her healing process required her to release her mother and to take proper care of herself. The spirits of her mother and father realized this, making an effort to help her take the first step. Released, her mother's spirit would no longer be anchored here, and Faye would be free to move forward with her own life, balancing her feelings without depending on food.

HAZEL WAS A sweet, lovely woman who was a civil law client of mine years ago. One day, Hazel stopped by my office unexpectedly to ask a legal question.

"I don't know why, but I felt directed to come here to talk to you, Mr. Anthony."

I thought to myself that a spirit must be up to something. I welcomed her into my office and asked how she had been.

Hazel did have a legal question on her mind, but somehow I felt she had more to ask. "What's wrong, Hazel? You look so sad."

She answered, "My mother passed six months ago. I miss her terribly."

"Would it help to talk about it?" I asked.

"I know my mother is at peace, but the problem is I'm not. I just can't accept her death."

"There's more, isn't there, Hazel?" I queried.

"Mr. Anthony, my church teaches that the dead know nothing, for they are asleep until Judgment Day. This is no consolation to me; I wish it was."

I replied, "With all due respect to your religion, I beg to differ about the dead knowing nothing."

"Mr. Anthony, I have known you a long time, and I respect you. Please tell me what you mean by that." She sat back in her chair.

I explained, "I am a medium, and ever since you walked into my office, I felt someone on the Other Side was trying to get a message through to you. However, I respect your beliefs, and I don't want to cross a line."

Hazel thought for a moment. "No, I want to hear what this person wants to say."

Hazel's mother was a Jamaican woman of small stature. She wore little wire-framed glasses and kept her steely gray hair tightly cropped. When she came through, she was wearing purple.

In my clairvoyant symbol language, the color purple indicates that the person had been very spiritual. Hazel's mother showed me a black leather Bible to indicate she was of a Christian faith. A brother who had died in his fifties accompanied her. The symptoms he communicated to me indicated he died quickly from a heart attack. He was a chubby man who seemed to have quite a sense of humor.

Hazel was somewhat taken aback but confirmed that I had accurately described her mother and her uncle.

"These two spirits are showing me bananas," I explained.

Hazel chuckled and said, "My mother believed in eating a banana a day for good health."

"Well, your mother also feels you need to eat more fresh fruits and vegetables to protect your health," I continued, relaying her mother's message.

Hazel stated, "My doctor is concerned about my cardiovascular health and has said my diet requires more fresh fruits and vegetables."

"They say you need more love in your life. They know that night after night you sit in a recliner brooding."

Hazel answered defensively, "Well, it's not every night I sit there, but most nights I do. I miss my mother terribly. Sometimes I wonder if I might be suffering from depression."

It was clear that her mother and uncle felt her pain and wanted to help. "They're showing me an image of a little dog, and I'm hearing the phrase, 'Get a dog.'"

Hazel's eyes opened wide. "How could they know I was thinking of getting a little dog?" She burst out laughing. "I need something to love and keep me company."

"Your mother is showing me a pink Valentine-type heart, which means she loves you—and now I'm also seeing the image of a white dove. Here, the white dove comes with a clairaudient message: 'Be at peace,'" I conveyed.

"I do need to find peace with her passing," Hazel said, "for my own good."

Moving forward with your life does not have to involve major changes. It may simply mean accepting the reality of what has taken place and giving yourself permission to feel love again.

For Hazel, bringing more opportunity to love into her life was what she needed, apparently. Feeling love again in the new love for a pet may help her find the path to inner peace. If a pet could help you to love again, then getting a companion animal certainly could be well worth the effort. You may even want to get your pet from an animal shelter and rescue it from being euthanized. If you've lost a life, then perhaps you can save a life.

IN MANY READINGS, pets come through and make contact. This leads to the question of whether animals have souls. Every living thing has an energy field that makes it alive. We can measure the electrical field of the brain and the heart. In physics, the second law of thermodynamics states that energy can neither be created nor destroyed, only transferred. Animals have a life force, and their energy goes somewhere when they physically die. When an animal dies, its energy field does not cease to exist; rather, it is transferred to the Other Side.

Do animals communicate with us from the Other Side? It is my belief that anyone and anything capable of love is capable of spirit communication. The key is whether the animal was capable of love. Love is an eternal force that transcends time, space, and physical death.

Animals might be much more sophisticated emotionally than we realize. I consider forgiveness and reconciliation virtues that require human reasoning. However, it appears that these qualities are not limited to just humans.

During a reading with Susie, her father, who had been a general in the United States Army, came through and was accompanied by the spirit of a German shepherd. A general accompanied by what I assumed was his German shepherd seemed normal, and initially I didn't grasp the significance of the dog's presence.

Susie looked perplexed. "What can you tell me about this German shepherd?"

"He had a very distinctive black snout," I explained. "Your father is petting the German shepherd, and the dog is wagging his tail."

"That's Sam, my sister's German shepherd. He had a very black snout. It's strange he came with my dad," Susie said.

"Why?"

"Dad hated that dog, and the dog seemed to hate him. Sam always growled at Dad when he came home, and Dad always threatened to have Sam put down. The two of them just didn't get along."

"Looks like they've made up on the Other Side," I replied.

"I guess all dogs really do go to Heaven," Susie added lightheartedly.

Love is a highly sophisticated emotion that isn't limited just to human beings. Anything capable of love is capable of spirit communication. Mammals and birds, which are both warm blooded, experience the emotion of love and are therefore able to communicate from the Other Side. The capability of love also makes them capable of another highly sophisticated ability: forgiveness. This reading demonstrated how two spirits, one of a human and one of a dog, were able to reconcile on the Other Side.

I've yet to connect with non-warm-blooded life forms that do not appear to be capable of love, such as snakes, spiders, alligators, and sharks. As interesting as connecting with cold-blooded creatures might be, in all honesty, I'd prefer not to. But as a medium, I must remain open-minded. So I'll just say that one never knows what is possible.

FOR SPIRITS WHO do express love, the last thing they want is for a loved one to suffer. Some people become so entrenched in grief that they neglect their own health, becoming emotionally numb. This is what your loved ones on the Other Side do not want. They feel your pain and want to console you. In essence, this anchors them to you. Unless you open up and communicate with them or allow your faith or belief system to guide you to inner peace, you are doing them and yourself a dreadful disservice.

While many people grieve intensely, others shut down their feelings in an attempt to avoid feeling pain. This emotional numbing becomes insulation from a painful memory. The suppression of emotions can result in someone being unable to experience joy and presents a double-edged sword, as it can also suppress positive feelings.

SPIRITS ARE ALWAYS attentive to what is going on in a loved one's life. When there is a problem needing a spirit's assistance, the spirit will come to the rescue and work with the loved one's spirit guide and spirit helpers. A spirit never abandons a loved one, as David came to understand.

David is an extremely gifted man. Over the course of his life he has been and continues to be an artist, poet, writer, museum curator, and professional orchid cultivator. David is also a veteran of the Vietnam War who suffers from depression and posttraumatic stress disorder. We met for lunch to discuss some business matters, and during our meal, I kept feeling spiritual entities reaching out to him. Since a busy restaurant is not the ideal place for a reading, I suggested we visit a nearby nature preserve. We found a shady spot and sat down.

David's mother had passed of Alzheimer's disease nearly a year before. It was clear there was a strong love connection between David and his mother.

"Before she died, she didn't even recognize me," David told me.

"She does now, and she wants you to know that she no longer suffers," I explained.

Although she was in her nineties when she passed, she looked about forty years old when her presence came in. Her sense of style seemed to reflect the 1960s. I described the type of cat-eye glasses she wore and her bouffant hairstyle.

David smiled. "Yeah, that sounds like Mom to me."

Next his father came through. "Your father looks like a man from the 1950s. He is appearing with a flat-top buzz haircut, a gray blazer, white shirt, dark slacks, and black tie."

David eyed me keenly. "So far, so good. Keep going."

"Your father was a serious person and a good man but one who was very much a nuts-and-bolts kind of guy."

"He was an engineer," David stated. "That's why we moved to Florida and lived in Titusville, near Kennedy Space Center."

"He is extending his right hand as if to shake hands but concealing his left hand behind his back. I don't understand this. Something about his left hand—he doesn't want people to see it," I said, somewhat perplexed.

David smiled. "My father's left hand was badly mangled in a farming accident, and he lost three fingers. He was always self-conscious about having what he felt was a deformity."

"I get the impression he felt awkward as a father," I conveyed. "He wasn't good at expressing his feelings."

"That's for sure," David indicated.

"He wants you to know he loved you and still does," I said.

"I know. He just wasn't open about his feelings," David replied.

David's maternal grandmother came through next. "She is a physically small woman wearing a shawl and eyeglasses, with close-cropped gray hair. She is showing me a ball of yarn, a gray tabby cat, and a barn with rolling green hills in the background," I described.

David confirmed, "She was from rural Pennsylvania, had lots of cats, and spent a lot of time knitting."

"These three spirits are working together to help you heal," I said.

David's intense gaze fixed upon me. "Heal? In what way?"

"You often feel alone, isolated, and ...," I paused.

"And?" David asked.

"They are concerned that you are contemplating suicide— often," I said, feeling somewhat uneasy.

David sat in silence for a moment and then looked up. "That's true. I'm constantly grappling with impulsive feelings that tell me to just end it all. I know Vietnam was a long time ago, but I've never been at peace since then. A lot of days, I just don't want to go on. But somehow, I always seem to find the strength to hang on."

"That is how they are helping you," I told him. "What they want you to know is that this impulsiveness and depression coupled with suicidal thoughts are obstacles you *must* overcome. These are life lessons you are here to learn."

"You mean they're helping me in this struggle?" David asked. "Is that possible?"

I told him what the spirits were telling me. "Absolutely. The spirits of your parents and grandmother want you to know they love you. They are standing by to help with your internal struggles. They know each time you're confronted with thoughts of suicide and are there to help you reject those impulses. This is making you stronger."

"Sort of like the old Nietzsche quote, 'That which does not kill us makes us stronger'?" David joked.

"They want you to know it is the battle *within* you that you must conquer in order to learn the lesson of coping with depression," I said as the reading ended. Before the spirits of David's relatives receded from my perception, they showed me white doves—clairvoyant symbols of peace.

David sat silently, apparently taking in what he'd just heard. Then he said, "It's true, then: we're never really alone, are we?"

"No, we aren't," I confirmed.

David required inner peace. His family members were there to guide him through the difficult journey and to give him the strength to resist taking his own life.

MERMAID GIFTS IS a store in downtown Melbourne, Florida, that specializes in the sale of unique items of a spiritual nature. It is owned by my friend Kim Cruickshank, an extremely positive, upbeat, and inspirational woman, who is originally from England. One day while we were talking about spirit contact, Kim asked if I would conduct a series of mediumship readings at Mermaid. I was happy to oblige my friend's request.

Kim scheduled several readings on a Saturday. One of these was for a fifteen-year-old girl, Maggie. Maggie had a Goth look—black eye makeup, black clothes with silver zippers and buttons, black fishnet stockings, and black leather boots. She was somewhat skeptical of spirit contact but said she was open-minded. Although I don't normally conduct readings for teenagers, she assured me there was no problem.

I felt a spiritual presence come through immediately. "I see a young man with blond hair. He is boyish in his demeanor. He has a kind and gentle disposition and is sensitive emotionally. It seems as if he was younger than you are now when he passed, Maggie."

Maggie's jaw dropped, and she brought her hand in front of her mouth.

"He passed suddenly. There was something wrong with his mind prior to passing. He felt disoriented, as if his brain wasn't functioning properly." I felt tightness in his chest, as if the problem with his head had precipitated cardiac arrest. From the experience of many readings, I understood this manner of death all too well.

Tears came to Maggie's eyes as she said, "I watched him die of a drug overdose right in front of me. This happened about a year and a half ago."

"He says he is so sorry," I conveyed. "He wants to ask your forgiveness."

"He wants *my* forgiveness? Maybe I could've done something to stop it. We were at a party, and he kept taking more and more. Why didn't I do something?" Maggie's eyes begged for an answer.

"This young man is reaching out to you emotionally. He doesn't want you to be so torn up. He wants to reassure you. It was not your fault. There wasn't anything you could have done to change things."

"Really?" she asked.

"Yes," I communicated the spirit's response. "Now he is showing me images of his funeral. So many people were there. The church was filled to capacity. He is sorry for how his death impacted so many others. He is showing me his mother crying and grieving so deeply for him."

"She was totally crushed," Maggie said. "We all were."

The next images he projected were unsettling. This young man's spirit showed me images of pills and a liquor bottle.

Then I received a message of warning from the spirit, which I conveyed to Maggie. "There is someone you haven't met yet who will remind you of this boy's spirit when he was alive. Because this man will seem familiar, you will trust this man when you shouldn't."

Maggie was perplexed. "I'm not sure I understand."

"Maggie, I don't like to get into forecasting the future; however, my job is to tell you whatever information the spirit transmits. Your friend wants you to know that if you trust this man and let him influence you, it could lead to drug and alcohol abuse, which then might lead to an overdose."

"I'm always careful!" Maggie protested.

"His warning is clear: beware of this situation. Remember, whoever this person is, he is *not* like your boyfriend on the Other Side."

"Wow! I was totally not expecting this." Maggie let out a deep breath.

"If you heed his warning, he says you should have a long and healthy life," I relayed. "However, you must let go of the remorse and regret from this young man's death. It is holding you back from healing and growing."

"So is he, like, saying I'm going to overdose?" Maggie looked concerned.

"No," I explained. "What he is saying is that a *potential* situation may arise that could put you in the wrong place at the wrong time. Whether or not this will come to pass is up to your free will. This spirit is persistent about a possible threat to your safety. It is up to you to be aware. Do not allow yourself to be swayed by others into doing something you know to be dangerous."

The spirit then showed me a shared memory. "The two of you attended a carnival. He cautiously put his arm around you, and then he blushed."

Maggie laughed and rolled her eyes. "He was so shy."

"He wants you to know he describes that as one of the happiest moments of his life."

"Yeah, he finally got the nerve to ask me out," Maggie smiled.

"He also shows how you were eating candy apples and other food." I described the images for her.

"Yeah, it was such a good time," Maggie said wistfully.

"I'm hearing the word *munchies,* and he is showing me marijuana," I told her. I knew the term *munchies* was slang for the food craved as a result of the voracious appetite induced by marijuana usage. This spirit had an interesting way of making his point.

"Oops," Maggie giggled.

"He doesn't want you to do to your mom what he did to his mother," I relayed. Then the spirit switched focus. "Since his death, he knows you and your mother are not getting along. Your mother is worried that what happened to him will happen to you."

"Yeah, we argue a lot. Mom is just such a total control freak." Maggie made a face.

"He feels you are being resistant to your mother. He says you must trust her and have a little more patience."

"I would like us to get along better. She just, you know, is always on my case," Maggie said.

"He wants you to know that it is important to get past any problems with your mother and to trust her. You must learn to communicate in a different way with her," I explained.

"Okay. I get it." Maggie sighed. "This was weird. Kind of cool, though."

AFTER MAGGIE LEFT, I continued conducting readings. Two people later, Tanya, an attractive, middle-aged woman, arrived.

Her father came through first. "He seems like an organized and mathematically oriented person. I get the feeling he might have been an engineer."

"Yes, he was," Tanya acknowledged.

"You and your father had a wonderful father-daughter relationship. Even when you disagreed with each other, it never ended in anger or animosity. The logical discussions you shared resolved any problems."

"That's true," Tanya said. "He always treated me like his intellectual equal. I miss him so much. I've never been able to talk to anyone like I could talk to Dad."

"This logical relationship brought your father great joy. He wants you to know he cherished your rapport," I conveyed.

Next, a young man's spirit appeared.

"There's a young man's spirit here, and he doesn't feel like a son, but he appears to have some connection with you..."

That's odd; this spirit seems so familiar. Whoa! It's the teenage boy who appeared during Maggie's reading!

"By any chance, did your daughter come to see me earlier today?"

"Yes," Tanya replied. "My daughter, Maggie, was here earlier."

"This is interesting. A young man is here, and he wants to communicate with you," I said, describing his appearance to her.

"Oh dear! From your description, I know exactly who you're talking about. It's Maggie's boyfriend. He died from a drug overdose." Tanya looked worried. "Why is he here?"

"He wants to apologize for bringing so much sorrow to so many people's lives. He is particularly sorry for upsetting Maggie and you so much. He knows that you fear what happened to him will happen to Maggie," I told her.

"Not a day goes by that I don't think about that," Tanya nodded.

"This young man wants to help," I said.

"How can he help? I've tried to talk to Maggie about drugs and about what happened to him. She just won't listen. She is unbelievably headstrong. She is intelligent and a good student, but I just can't get through to her!" Tanya's face mirrored her frustration.

This was an ethical dilemma that I knew had to be handled carefully and diplomatically. I didn't want to alarm this woman by saying this spirit had warned Maggie about trusting someone she shouldn't who might lead her down the deadly path of a drug overdose. On the other hand, this could become an extremely serious situation. In a case like this, a medium must trust the spirits. They are here to help, not to harm.

"Let's ask him how he can help," I said, focusing on the young man's spirit. "Maybe he can offer useful advice."

"By all means," Tanya agreed.

"He suggests you change your strategy in communicating with Maggie. Try not to talk down to her, and don't scare her. Communicate in a nonthreatening way."

"Okay," Tanya said nervously. "It's just that I'm terribly worried about her."

"The spirit feels your concerns are justified; however, without realizing it, you are clamping down on Maggie. Instead of drawing her closer, you're pushing her away."

"I've felt this happening, but I haven't known what to do." Tanya's face reflected her concern.

Suddenly the spirit of Tanya's father chimed back in. "Your father says to communicate with Maggie on an adult level and in a logical fashion—the way he communicated with you. The young man's spirit agrees."

"Dad is working with this boy?" Tanya asked.

"It's clear these two spirits came through in tandem to convey this message. It is up to both you and Maggie to learn to communicate with each other differently. By doing this, maybe you will be able to avoid potential problems," I explained.

"Problems? What types of problems?" Tanya asked nervously. "Do you mean drugs?"

Her father's spirit once again took the lead. "Maggie will listen to you about drugs once you start treating her like an adult. This will create a more secure bond based on love instead of fear," I conveyed.

"Hmm... I do try to scare her about drugs. I suppose I'm overcompensating. I've just been so afraid since that boy died. I've had no peace of mind. His mother was devastated. My heart breaks just thinking about her!"

Tanya continued, "Since that happened, I guess I haven't given Maggie the respect my dad gave to me. I'm trying to shelter her, and she's pulling away."

The young man's spirit came forward again, emphasizing Tanya's father's advice. "Speak to her through love, not fear. By acting out of fear, you'll drive her away. Act out of love, and you'll gain her trust."

"He was such a kind boy. Please thank him for still caring about Maggie," Tanya requested. Then she exclaimed, "And thank you, Dad! You've never let me down. I love you!"

While Maggie's mother's concerns were justified, her fear-based concern caused Maggie to resent her, resulting in emotional distance. But spirits came to the rescue of Maggie and her mother. Both women were presented with messages concerning communication based on love and trust instead of fear and anger. If they can learn to communicate with each other differently, then their rapport as mother and daughter may improve. Perhaps they will also come to accept the passing of this young man and find inner peace.

WHEN SOMEONE YOU love passes, feelings of fear, sorrow, and anguish often accompany that person's death. Realizing that you will never see that person in physical form again, and fearing that you could have done something to prevent that person's death, hits hard. You may blame yourself, anguishing that you didn't show enough love. Or, if the last words between you were unkind, you may be haunted by that fact. Perhaps the worst fear of all is that your loved one has simply vanished and no longer exists.

Fear is a creation of the human ego. Fear, though, is not necessarily a bad thing. Fear can be a deterrent to dangerous behaviors. A healthy fear of sticking your hand in a fire is a good thing. However, when not tempered by common sense and love, fear can have disastrous results.

As an attorney, I've learned that fear is the root of many criminal acts. Criminals often feel they are not in control of their lives. Many crimes are committed by someone trying to satisfy an ego by feeling powerful and in control. As a medium, I've seen that many people fear that nothing exists beyond this life. Fear can lead to depression, which can, in turn, lead to substance abuse, alcoholism, and impulsive behaviors.

What dies when we die is the human ego and the negativity caused by fear. Spirits in the Light on the Other Side are not fearful or angry. They are freed from fear and all negative emotions.

God's gift is love. Love is eternal. Love is created by God to sustain us in times of sorrow. We are all connected to the life force of God and God's spiritual energy. In essence, we are immortal spiritual beings created in the image of God.

As people, we experience the material world. When the physical aspect of this experience is completed, we return to our spiritual form. We are all cells in the spiritual body of God, created in the mind of God, and we return there to the source of unconditional love.

Do not mistake unconditional love with desire. It is possible to fall in love with a person and have it lead to disastrous results. The divorce rate alone is evidence of this. The love I address is one without conditions. This is love offered with no expectations in return.

Unconditional love is the basis for positive emotions: love for family and friends, love of life, and love for self. Loving others as you love yourself brings joy to all around you. You can only experience happiness when you are filled with love. Love is a powerful force that shows us the Light in times of darkness. We heal through love in times of loss. It is through love that we feel the presence of God. It is love that allows us to receive the love of spirits who are on the Other Side.

Working through fear, rage, guilt, anger, and resentment is a necessary part of the grieving process. However, these fear-based feelings must not control one's life. The reality of physical death must be accepted. What must be changed is one's perspective on death.

While living in the material world, we are subject to all of the pain and physical limitations of a material existence. We live, we love, we suffer, and we die physically. The reason we must endure these things is to learn the lessons that accompany these experiences. Understanding this does not make coping with the loss of a loved one any less painful. However, learning to cope is an important part of our material experience. It's our job.

Accepting that death is not the end is key to finding inner peace. All of the great faiths of the world teach us that death begins the continuation of our soul's journey. The mission of a medium is to help people realize this by facilitating a connection with their loved ones on the Other Side, relaying messages of love, forgiveness, redemption, joy, and fulfillment.

Life is a river, and we must flow with it, not against it. When the waters become turbulent, we have to rise above the turbulence and accept what we cannot change. This does not mean giving up or surrendering to grief. This means moving forward and doing our best to calm the waters.

Many people allow the turbulence and emotional conflict caused by death to dominate their lives, replacing all other emotions. Inner peace is blocked.

Spirits know this and do not want us to suffer. They will reach out to each of us from a place of great love and forgiveness. The spirit world wants us to understand that love is eternal.

I know this from my own experience. My mother, Jeannie, told me from the Other Side how to accept her passing and find inner peace: "Let go of the sorrow, but hold on to the love."

Every time I think of this message, it makes me smile. After all, a mom would never let something like death get in the way of telling her son what to do.

13

Let Go of Sorrow, Hold On to Love

S pirits can and do come to our rescue by reaching out to help us let go of the sorrow but hold on to the love. This may be the most profound message I have received from the Other Side. Letting go of the sorrow and of all the pain associated with death doesn't cure grief, but it can place it in a new perspective. Holding on to the love for the person who passed allows the shock and trauma of the death to subside and painful memories to be replaced by happier ones.

For me, mediumship has been a blessing through which I have come to the understanding that death is not the end. The knowledge that those who have died are not gone forever has brought me great comfort. I find tremendous joy in knowing God exists and that there truly is spiritual life after physical life. Now my mission in life is to assist others in finding that same peace after the passing of their loved ones.

Understanding that death is not the end cannot make the grieving process painless. No one is ever really prepared for the death of a loved one. It always hurts. In some instances, death may seem to bring relief from a prolonged terminal illness, but it is still painful. An emptiness is created in our home and in our heart. Many times death is a shock because it was totally unexpected.

The death of a child is excruciatingly difficult to process. This is the most agonizing loss. It is natural for the older to predecease those who are young. However, when a child dies, it is as if the natural order of our universe has been shattered in the worst way. Many bereaved parents suffer, saying over and over, "This wasn't supposed to happen. This is not the way it should be. It isn't fair!"

Grief is the price of love. If you were fortunate enough to love, the death of a loved one brings a depth of pain proportionate to your love. This loss is a truly heavy cross to bear. Accepting the loss, processing it, and learning to live and even to be happy again is difficult. Loss changes everyone.

By truly accepting death and enduring the grieving process, the waves of pain become less frequent and the ability to cope will exceed their intensity. You will become a stronger person. That does not mean you will be immune to feeling, but the process will increase the depth of your capacity for emotions. You will have a higher appreciation of love. You will cherish the intense happiness that no one is guaranteed but that everyone is capable of experiencing. You will hold the good and the beautiful more dearly, and you will have more compassion for those who are suffering. As Jesus said, "Blessed are those who mourn, for they shall be comforted."

Of course, I cannot address all the mysteries of the universe, but I do know with certainty that when the physical body expires, the spiritual energy of the soul lives on. It leaves the physical body—the breath of life, the electricity of the heartbeat and brain—and takes the consciousness, the distinct personality, the memories, and the love with it. In other words, the energy is you. When you die, you take *you* with you.

That is why it is important to understand that when a loved one dies, the relationship does not. As I've said before, it evolves into one of a purely spiritual nature. Your loved one's life mission here has been completed, and the soul has elevated to another plane of existence in the spiritual realm. That is why the message to let go of the sorrow but hold on to the love has so much meaning.

We all know the grieving process is complex, replete with myriad negative feelings such as fear, anger, guilt, despair, outrage, and hopelessness. And we must understand that this pain does not go unnoticed by the spirit of the person who passed.

Due to the connection created by our love, a spirit can be tethered to us when he or she feels our excessive grief, wanting to reach out and let us know that he or she is fine and happy. The desire to communicate this sentiment can anchor a spirit here, reluctant to leave us suffering even as this may keep the spirit from ascending higher into the Light.

Unresolved grief issues are problematic enough for the living. They also cause problems for spirits. Spirits are not stagnant, much less floating around on clouds, playing harps. They have a whole new life on the Other Side that includes additional lessons and missions. Physical death is not the end of growth for spirits; they continue to evolve and learn. We must not hold them back from engaging in their new life on the Other Side.

Death should be viewed as the transference of energy from a material existence to a spiritual one. Since we are spiritual beings having a material experience, it is a natural progression that, when our material existence is complete, we return to the spiritual plane. Although a true understanding of the Other Side may be beyond our comprehension, this new experience appears to be blissful, peaceful, and happy.

Spirits are happy to be freed of the burden of a human body, with all of its limitations, ailments, and problems. Even though a spirit may have unresolved issues with people here, I've never met a spirit that regretted being on the Other Side. Consider this analogy: if you could ask a butterfly if it would like to be a caterpillar again, what do you think the butterfly's response would be?

This does not mean for a second that anyone should intentionally cut life short. We are here to move through the experiences in this life. Terminating a life early takes away the benefits of the life lessons we are all here to learn.

I have conducted numerous readings for people whose loved ones have committed suicide. The spirits assure me that condemnation to eternal damnation does not happen. What they do experience is the heavy burden of unfinished business that must be resolved with loved ones here. These spirits came through to apologize for causing so much pain to those they left behind. While this apology may not wipe away the pain or suffering of the survivors, it is an important step in the healing process for them—and for the evolution of the spirit.

One spirit told me, "Suicides have to come back."

I pressed the spirit to explain what he meant by this statement. Did this mean come back spiritually to make amends, or did it mean to reincarnate?

"Both," the spirit replied.

Instead of ascending into the Light to become aligned with the higher frequency of God's love, a person who commits suicide may be required to come back here to take on again the life lessons they did not learn. However, the new lessons will be more challenging because this person must deal with both old baggage and new.

Life is full of lessons that will be repeated until they are learned. The life lessons become more difficult and more complex each time one must have a do-over. You can only imagine what you might have to deal with the next time. We are spiritual entities who are connected to a body to learn these lessons. We must realize there is a larger life plan, and we are participants in it.

WHAT IS THE reason for our existence? What sense is there to life? Why do so many people have to suffer, while others seem to have a luxurious life without working or suffering? Why? Once again, I believe the answer came to my mother, who was plagued by many tragedies and serious medical conditions throughout her life.

I came home from college one day during spring break. My mother greeted me. She had a beautiful and serene look in her eyes. I recognized this as the expression she usually had after a major psychic episode. It was one of enlightenment, knowing, awe, and compassion.

"Mom, what happened to you today?" I asked.

She replied, "I had an extraordinary experience. I was in so much pain and so frustrated with being sick. I asked God why—why must I suffer? Does my life even matter?" She paused and then, with the utmost serenity, whispered, "I heard a voice. The voice said, 'It is all for death.'"

"That's kind of scary, Mom," I commented.

My mother continued, "No, it's not scary at all. I knew in an instant the voice was telling me that all life has meaning and value."

It seemed like a morbid message to me. She continued to explain. "Good, bad, or indifferent, we must get through our life here. We must endure what has been placed in our path and never intentionally end our life. What we do here affects us in the afterlife. That is why everything we do in life— everything we have to suffer or endure—is all for death."

With the startling revelation that everything we do in life is in preparation for life on the Other Side, my mother changed profoundly. Always a caring person, she became even more compassionate, affirming that every life counts and everyone matters. In retrospect, I believe that her psychic experience that day brought her stronger skills to cope with her own life challenges, of which she had many.

Our conversation continued. "Did you receive a message about why you have to suffer so much?" I asked. "It breaks my heart to see you in so much pain."

"I try not to dwell on my problems, Mark," my mother replied.

"You've been through so much. How can you be so strong?" I asked.

Her response carried some of the best advice I've ever received. "When you are sad and depressed, think of ten people you know. That doesn't mean movie stars you read about or personalities you see on TV but people you really know. Ask yourself, would you really want to change places with any of them? Do you want their problems, their pain, their ills and suffering? What about their family issues? Would you want any of that?"

I thought for a moment and said, "No, I wouldn't."

"Remember this, and it will help you appreciate who and what you are," she said.

"Wow! I never thought of it like that, Mom."

"You see, Mark, we are dealt a hand of cards to play in life. Some of the cards aren't good; some are bitter and difficult. Others are wonderful and loving. Life isn't supposed to be easy. It's a series of lessons, and sometimes the lessons are really tough. When you see those you think have it all, you don't know what pain they carry around. That's why we must be compassionate and kind to everyone." She smiled, and then added, "When life gives you lemons, make Italian lemon ice. That is what the message 'It is all for death' really means."

Mom helped me to understand that we are here to embrace everything that comes with life. The journey is often full of complex, difficult, and painful obstacles. How we deal with the obstacles and even the blessings will determine whether or not we have taken our life lessons to heart. Healing grief is one such lesson.

As a medium, I feel wonderful when I can help a hurt or grieving person make a connection with someone who has crossed over to the Other Side. It is a great honor and profound privilege to be permitted to assist in this important step toward healing.

While contact with a spirit through a medium can be a tool in the healing process, it does not remove all the pain and sense of loss. However, a medium may to some degree be able to assist a person in gaining a new perspective with the objective of the acceptance of death. This may lead to inner peace in the knowledge that the one who passed is now in God's Light. Despite this knowledge, and with my own ability to connect spiritually with my loved ones who have passed, I will always miss those I love.

Faith in God, psychic activity, mediumship, and contact with the spiritual realm are not the cure-all, but they are tools that help us find hope. Hope is the shining star in the dark night of sorrow, for faith in God brings inner strength, and spirit contact can bring hope and validation. In the final analysis, you must give yourself time and permission for the healing process to take place.

Sometimes we feel that by letting go of the sorrow, we are abandoning the memory or somehow dishonoring the deceased loved one: "If I stop hurting so much, will I forget?" While you never get over the loss, letting go of sorrow is essential. Hold fast to your love. This does not mean excluding a new love from coming into your life. We can still continue to love and honor the person who has passed.

It is important for our spiritual development while we are in the material world that we remain open to the lessons we are here to learn. We must do this work in the here and now. Procrastination has no rewards. You might consider life as school and death as graduation. You can take comfort in knowing that when you cross over to the Other Side, your loved ones will be there to greet you.

Maybe the readings I've been privileged to share can bring a new perspective to your sense of loss. In some instances, I know others who have had contact with a spirit without the benefit of a medium. Without realizing it, this may have happened to you, too.

Stop and remember some of your experiences since a loved one has passed. Did you notice any events similar to those chronicled in this book? Many people feel the presence of a loved one near. It is common to have a coherent dream in which the deceased visits. What about smelling a familiar scent associated with that person? Did you come home to find a photo album open to a picture of a person who has passed, and you can't imagine how that happened? Instinctively, you turn on the car radio just in time to hear a song that brings back a vivid memory of someone on the Other Side. Contact experiences are real.

Remember what faith teaches you. God exists. The Other Side exists. Our soul is an immortal living spirit. We can communicate with the spirits of loved ones. We will be reunited with our loved ones on the Other Side. When we die physically, our soul lives on. We do not cease to exist. Once we cross to the Other Side, we continue to progress and evolve.

I WOULD LIKE to leave you with a message from the Other Side that I was privileged to communicate to Veronica.

It was a hot, humid August day in Florida. I was presenting a lecture on mediumship and life after death at Kasey Claytor's Osprey Meditation Center in Titusville. At the end of the lecture, I conducted a series of readings for members of the audience.

"A young man is coming through. He was very mischievous when he was a boy. He liked to pull pranks and surprise his mother. He didn't mean any harm by it. Does that make sense to anyone?" I asked.

No one raised a hand. Although the lack of a response was disheartening, this was a strong link, and I knew I had to have faith and trust in God. So I continued, "When he was in grade school, his mom always packed him a lunch. His favorite was a bologna sandwich—and he insisted on white bread, not whole wheat."

A woman raised her hand. "My name is Veronica. That's my son, Bill."

"What seems odd," I relayed, "is the cause of death. It was sudden. It feels like it was a drug overdose, but he doesn't seem to be the type of person to have been using illegal drugs."

This piece of information was obviously extremely difficult for her to hear. "Bill died of a drug overdose. He had a bad reaction to his prescription medications, and his heart stopped. When we realized what had happened, it was too late." She maintained her composure, although I could see she was straining to do so.

"He wants you to know that he saw you put up the mobile. It is the one with seashells. He made it, and now you have hung it up where you can enjoy it. He says whenever you look at it, think of him."

"Good heavens!" she exclaimed. "He made that mobile out of driftwood and shells he found on the beach. Since his death I just couldn't bring myself to hang it up. Last week I did. It brought me comfort to hold something he had made with his own hands. I was thinking of him when I did it."

I hesitated slightly before delivering the final message. At first blush, I felt it was a cliché and might sound contrived, but I knew the message wasn't coming from me. It was coming from the spirit to her through me. Once again, I knew I had to trust in God that this young man's spirit was communicating something important that needed to be said.

"He says, 'I give you the gift of everlasting peace.'"

No one in the room made a sound.

Finally, Veronica whispered, "Oh dear God." Tears flowed from her eyes as she began to weep. Two friends who were sitting on either side of her embraced her as she wept. All three of them began to cry. After several moments, Veronica looked up as she wiped the tears from her eyes and said, "Just two weeks before my son died, he wrote an article for our church newspaper."

As I gazed into her eyes, I could see some of the burden of her grief lifting as she spoke. "The title of his article was 'The Gift of Everlasting Peace.'"

Her son's spirit knew it was time to come to the rescue and help her let go of the sorrow but hold on to the love. To help her heal, he wanted her to have the gift of everlasting peace.

And in the journey through grief, could any of us hope for more?

There is something beyond this life,
and it is wonderful!

—Rocco Aurena

Acknowledgments

I have been blessed to have so many amazing people be part of my journey, who also were instrumental in the writing of this book. I would especially like to acknowledge my father, Earl; my sister, Roxanne; and my brother, Earl Joseph, for not only always loving me but for being my best friends. To my niece, Laura, and my nephew, Earl, thanks for keeping me looking to the future.

Special thanks to my literary agents Jeff Herman and Deborah Herman of the Jeff Herman Agency. Thank you to Carrie Obry and the entire staff at Llewellyn Publications, and to my dear friend, the quintessential New Yorker, Katharine Sands.

I'm grateful for my extended family: Nancy and Mel Rowe, Sue Rice, James Goodman, Evelyn Tallman and the entire Tallman family, Reverend April Rane, Elaine Christine, David Swoyer, Alan Anter, Louise Kleba, Roger Pierce, Stephanie Rolls, Marina Baratian, Gail Baratian, Dawn Schnuck, Judy Powers, Sharon Williams, Frank Rash, Michael Rosenberg, Melanie Herz, Andrea Rosenberg, Roni Welton, Steven G. Casanova Esq., Vicki Rios-Martinez, and Mitch and Joan Needelman.

Thank you Melissa Olds, Amy Akbas, Kevin Roberts, Cheri Hart, Teren Nichols, Joseph Epplett, Ellen Cameron, Susan Rizzo, Michael McCarthy, Kim Cruickshank, Amy Hendricks, Bridget Hull, Hildegarde Cochran, Anthony Angolia, Bonnie Gautreau, Kelley Dunn, Ann Dunn, Mary Howard, Anita Carbone, General Michael J. Carey and Melody Carey, Muse Ritter, Sandy Venditti, Ardy Skinner, Alexia Hemmingway, Nancy Ambrosini, Amirah Hall, Andrea de Michaelis, Heidi Arapa and all my other good friends from the land down under, Marty and Juan Joyce (since I've seen you on the Other Side, Marty, I guess I won the argument about the existence of an afterlife), Kasey Claytor, Holly Vellekoop, Judith Mammy, and Pat McDonough.

I cannot express my gratitude enough to the tutors, staff, and students of the Arthur Findlay College for the Advancement of Psychic Science in Stansted, England. I consider the college my second home. Special thanks to Reverend Val Williams, Eamonn Downey, Jan Marshall, Reverend Judith Seaman, Morag Bence, and their counterpart in America, Marilyn Jenquin. Thank you to my UK psychic friends: Jane Dawson, Angel Anne Smith, and Simon Milton-Jones (the Highlander who somehow ended up at the Arctic Circle in Norway).

The friendship of my fellow psychics and mediums has truly been a gift from God. Thank you Lydia Clar, Jeffrey Wands, Chuck Bergman, Robert Brown, Morgana Starr, Willow Crystal, Anne Miller, Pamela Nine, Don McIntosh, Dikki-Jo Mullen, Jorie Eberle, Lori Kirwan, John Rogers, Patricia Quinn, and Reverend Pat Raimondo.

I've been privileged to work with so many incredible people in the media who have become friends, especially an amazingly gifted visionary and producer, Glenda Shaw, and her accomplice in creativity and TV production, Lora Wiley.

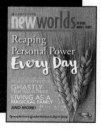

To Write to the Author

If you wish to contact the author or would like more information about this book, please write to the author in care of Llewellyn Worldwide, and we will forward your request. Both the author and the publisher appreciate hearing from you and learning of your enjoyment of this book and how it has helped you. Llewellyn Worldwide cannot guarantee that every letter written to the author can be answered, but all will be forwarded. Please write to:

Mark Anthony
℅ Llewellyn Worldwide
2143 Wooddale Drive
Woodbury, MN 55125-2989
Please enclose a self-addressed stamped envelope for reply,
or $1.00 to cover costs. If outside the USA, enclose
international postal reply coupon.

Many of Llewellyn's authors have websites with additional information and resources. For more information, please visit our website:

HTTP://WWW.LLEWELLYN.COM

Let go of the sorrow,
but hold on to the love.

—Jeannie Anthony